D0461880

The Confident Woman

ANABEL GILLHAM

HARVEST HOUSE PUBLISHERS
Eugene, Oregon 97402

THE CONFIDENT WOMAN
Copyright ©1993 by Anabel Gillham
Published by Harvest House Publishers
Eugene, Oregon 97402

Library of Congress Cataloging-in-Publication Data

Gillham, Anabel.
    The confident woman / Anabel Gillham
        p. cm.
    Rev. ed. of: A woman's strength.
    Includes bibliographical references.
    ISBN 1-56507-071-2
    1. Women—Religious life. 2. Marriage—Religious aspects—Christianity. 3. Gillham, Anabel. I. Gillham, Anabel. Woman's strength.
II. Title.
BV4527.G55 1993
248.8'43—dc20   93-19
                                                                  CIP

———— ❧❦❧ ————

To the Men in My Life,
In the Order of Their Appearance
On the Stage:

Marcus Hoyle, My Dad
Jesus Christ, My Lord
Bill Gillham, My Husband
and
My Four Sons:
Preston, Mason, Will, and Wade

Acknowledgments

I would like to acknowledge three people especially for the part they played in this production.

My husband, Bill, who has been my principal mentor through our years together.

My son, Will, who read and reread the original manuscript and gave me his invaluable editing advice.

And Susan Endsley, for the marvelous contribution she made in the study guide and for her dedication and enthusiasm for the wonderful message of our identity in Christ.

I needed all of you and I thank you. I love you.

Contents

When All Else Fails...

I had finally come to the point of complete desperation. I turned to God with one thought in mind, one conviction: I can't go on this way. The bared, soft, searching heart—broken. He knew. He saw. Why try to hide? "God, show me. Teach me. I've got to know...."

For 20 years—long years—I had tried to be everything my husband, Bill, wanted me to be. I had corrected every fault he pointed out and tried to change my personality to suit him, but it wasn't working. I was hurting, hating myself and the circumstances that had finally proven to be too much for me.

That took a lot of "doing." I was strong. During those 20 years my ability to endure had been severely tested. Each of our children, from boy one to boy four, was born into physical adversity (the Gillham family was well-known in the pediatric wards of the local hospitals). Mason, our second son, had a physical impairment that could not be corrected—he was profoundly retarded. Financial problems? Big ones, but I can handle them. In-law problems? I can work them out. Heavy household decisions? I can manage. Through my bootstrap efforts, *my* sheer determination, I had survived.

And yet, my marriage—indeed, my whole life—was so far from what I had always hoped it would be. I had come to see myself as helpless, my efforts as futile. I knew that God had promised life, *abundant* life, to those who follow Him. I knew what He intended for marriage to be. But here I was, a dedicated Christian—desiring God's will, God's best—simply enduring much of my life. My husband and I were growing farther and farther apart, building our own worlds, struggling to meet our needs in our own ways, and all the while passing on to our children the futility and frustration of our marriage.

As I look back on it all now, I am amazed that I was still standing after those 20 years. But there again, my super strength came through. You might think that had I ripped off my blouse there would have been a Wonder Woman suit underneath. But there was no Wonder Woman. It was only Anabel doing life in her own strength, strength that had never failed—up until that point in time.

* * *

There are so many things I want to share with you—truths I have discovered through the years, truths I would so wish you could come to know in *your* life. These truths are in this book only because the Holy

Spirit patiently taught them to me and tutored me into their realization. Once I saw them, everything began falling into place, and that's why I want them to become yours.

I know what God has done and is doing in my life—as a woman; as the wife of Bill Gillham; as the mother of Preston, Mason, Will, and Wade; as a counselor and lecturer. I am a disciple, seeking to know the will of God. I have realized my needs and I have discovered the source of their fulfillment. I have acknowledged my problems, and, by the grace of God, I am embracing the solution. And God compels me to share what He has shown me, not only because of what it has done in *my* life, but because of the extraordinary restoration it has brought about in other lives as well.

Women today are seeking. Most of us want desperately to know what God had in mind when He created the female. What is our role? Who are we, and how are we to be?

Yes, we've read books, sought counsel, heard sermons, attended seminars, and bought tapes. The problem is that we have come away inspired, enthusiastic, loaded with good intentions, ready, willing to change, and yet entirely unable to carry it all out: "How do I make it work? I've tried and I just can't do it!" What pure release it is for me now to utter those same words—"Lord, I can't"—because I have heard Him say, "Anabel, I *can.*"

I don't know you. I don't know what your life has been until now, what you have done or endured. Perhaps you're divorced or separated or widowed, and you are wondering what life holds for you now; maybe you're married, desiring fulfillment in your role as wife and mother; maybe you are alone and desperate, seeking direction and answers. Whatever your status, this book is for you. Read with an open heart and a willing mind.

Only the Holy Spirit can impart spiritual truths and enable you to incorporate them into your life. By His grace I will present them, but you alone can choose to take them up. Test what is written here. Go to the Bible. Ask God to give you wisdom to know and understand; ask Him to reveal the truth to you.

God has placed in every woman certain longings, certain needs, that are the same. We are kindred spirits, you and I, and my prayer is that you will come to know His indescribable love for you and His intricate plan for your life as we journey together.

Lovingly,
Anabel

PART I

Who I Am in Relation to Christ

1

Where Horses Belong

If you're serious about going somewhere, about making progress, then putting the cart before the horse will bring you nothing but frustration, futility, and possibly disaster.

First find out where the horse is supposed to be, then (so you won't always be asking questions) find out why the horse belongs there—and while you're at it, find out how to make him go. . . .

What does it take to put the cart before the horse? A lot of work!

First of all, once you finally persuade the horse to push instead of pull, you need someone holding up the tongue of the cart to keep it from digging into the ground. Surely you can figure a way to make this work.

You could rest the tongue on a round rock, I suppose. So you roll a few feet, stop, move the rock, and position the tongue again.

Of course, you have to entice the horse with something to make him go, like sugar cubes or carrots or hay. In a moment of brilliant insight, you decide not to try the hay because it would be hard to keep on a stick. You opt for the sugar cubes and carrots. It just makes so much more sense.

So here you are, all ready to go. But you're not *in* the cart! Nope, you're walking along beside the cart, dangling your bait from a stick in front of the horse's mouth, feeding him a sugar cube every once in a while to keep him going.

But you still have a *big* problem: The horse starts pushing, takes three or four steps, and the wagon tongue noses into the ground again. You take some time to study this a bit longer. How about a wheel on the tongue? Then it will roll on its own, and you can forget this rock-and-roll business! Ah, what ingenuity. Congratulations. Now you can at least *walk* at a steady pace; that is, as long as your bait holds out.

Quick! Someone run to the store and get some more sugar cubes. Find a longer stick for this carrot, too. And clean the dirt out of that wheel on the tongue—it's getting all clogged up again!

And with a considerable amount of hustle and bustle and frenzied activity, you're (sigh) moving right along.

This makes for quite a ridiculous picture, doesn't it? Why? Because we know where the horse belongs, what he's supposed to do, and how the cart is designed to work. That horse has to be in *front* of the cart before we can go anywhere. We've got to capitalize on *his* strength and stop trying to do things our way. Just think, we could be sitting in the cart, eating those carrots ourselves. We could let that horse do all the work for us. What a relief that would be.

How many of us—in our daily lives, in our Christian walk, in our marriages, as mothers, as employees—have the cart before the horse? Oh, there's a lot of effort and frenzied activity. We go from one meeting to another, from a Gothard seminar to a Dobson film, from a broken marriage to a therapist. We read every new book on the market, put forth every effort, and suddenly find ourselves so tired and beaten that we give up. We quit without ever realizing the magnificent, untapped power we have at our disposal.

I tried everything I knew to pull my life together (even hauling the horse myself I suppose!), and when I became so weary that I could not go on, when I was discouraged and *entirely* disillusioned, I finally allowed God to assume His position in my life. The cart and the horse changed places.

How desperate are you?

> *If this doesn't work, Anabel, I'm giving up. I can't—I won't—go on. Surely there is more to life than what I am living.*

Are you tired of the masks?

> *To everyone else we are a delightful, talented, dedicated family. But when the door closes behind us, we are nothing more than four people living in a house.*

Are you willing?

God, the Christian life is something You designed—it must be a good thing—but my life is so empty—so meaningless—hollow. Please God, show me what to do. Make something true and beautiful out of this mess. And use me—I'm willing.

Every woman who is searching for truth will eventually come to a personal Waterloo. What does that mean? That she will experience a "disastrous or decisive defeat." She'll come to the end of her own resources—the end of her ability to meet the circumstances that come into her life.

My Waterloo was my marriage—*the* overwhelming defeat that exhausted all my efforts and left me ravaged on the battlefield. That's when I began to search diligently (I had previously undertaken several halfhearted searches) through the Bible in order to find out what God said about marriage, and I encountered an admonition that was virtually *impossible* for me to carry out:

> Let the wife see that she respects and reverences her husband—that she notices him, regards him, honors him, prefers him, venerates and esteems him; and that she defers to him, praises him, and loves and admires him exceedingly (Ephesians 5:33b, AMP).

And I didn't even *like* my husband, much less all of those other things! Our marriage was not a good one, and no matter how hard I tried, it seemed to get worse instead of better. Of course, not a single soul knew that our marriage was anything short of perfect. I wasn't about to let anyone know—I could not endure the thought of someone knowing I was a failure at something that was my responsibility. But, oh, how I longed to be loved, to be cherished, to experience for myself the poetry of Robert Browning:

> Grow old along with me!
> The best is yet to be,
> The last of life, for which the first was made.

Was I expecting too much?

How about you? What is your frustration level? Where are your emotions? Are you trying to keep the facade of the "ideal" Christian couple in place, struggling like crazy to hold that "ideal" marriage together? Perhaps you're single . . . again. Your children live with you, and there are absolutely not enough hours in your day to be the provider and mom and dad and tutor and friend and housekeeper and cook and doctor and disciplinarian. You wonder where you'll get the strength to deal with the trauma of the circumstances that brought you into this unbelievable lifestyle. Or maybe you're a woman who's never been married. Day by day you find yourself growing more frustrated by what's *not* happening in your life.

Exploring our role as women—who we are and what we want—will be just as frustrating, futile, and disastrous as trying to "cart the horse," unless we first realize our position in Christ Jesus. I'm not talking about a position like marriage, or about the relationship of woman to man, but as a disciple to Christ, seeking to understand and embrace as our own plan His plan, and then going on to discover how to make that plan work.

What is it that we all long for? What do we, as women, *want*? For me, my dream was that my prince would come and we would meld into an inseparable oneness and maybe even "live happily ever after." A lovely fairy tale. I tried so hard to make that fairy tale come true.

But according to John 15:5, Jesus said, "Apart from Me, you can do *nothing*" (emphasis added). (*Nothing:* not any thing; that which does not exist; a nonentity; a thing, event, or remark of no account; absence of all magnitude or quantity; a zero.) Nothing? That's a sobering thought.

I want to argue with God. I want to say, "But, Lord, there *are* some things I can do quite well!" That's not the point. This is the basic plan, the rudimentary principle of His original intent: If I am incapable of doing a thing—if I can, indeed, do nothing—how much help do I need to get my life straightened out? To recreate my marriage? To face each pressure-filled moment? To do *anything?* You're right. I don't need someone to *help* me; I need someone to do it *all* for me.

It would be 42 long years before I realized the incredible, liberating wonder of this truth.

2

Somebody Loves Me

All I am or ever hope to be is in Him. Without Him, I am nothing. With Him, I am everything. And when I am not "everything"? He loves me still.

During the seven years Bill was a psychology professor at Southeastern Oklahoma State University, we lived in an old, two-story white house on Main Street. I loved to keep it up; it was almost like "playing house."

Early one fall I began to find little brown moths flying around, from the sunroom downstairs to the bath upstairs. I knew they were up to no good, so I killed them indiscriminately. It was a battle I could not win. They kept cropping up in the carpet, the closets, and the clothing. I finally came to the point where I had to admit that killing those moths one by one was not the answer. I had to get to the source, the *root* of the problem. I had to call in an expert and follow his advice.

And What Did He Say?

There are as many different heartaches in this world as there are women, but to broach each individual problem would not necessarily help us to get to the root of the dilemma, the underlying cause, the crumbling foundation. We need to call in the expert and follow His advice.

> Therefore every one who hears these words of Mine, and acts upon them, may be compared to a wise man, who built his house upon the rock. And the rain descended, and the floods came, and the winds blew, and burst against that house; and yet it did not fall, for it had been founded upon the rock. And every one who hears these words of Mine, and does not act upon them, will be like a foolish man, who built his house upon the sand. And the rain descended, and the floods came, and the winds blew, and burst against that house; and it fell, and great was its fall (Matthew 7:24-27).

For some of you, the rains have come, the winds have blown, and they have nearly destroyed you and all you hold dear. You need an answer, a solution. You can't go on—you may not even have the will to try.

For others, the rain has just started, and you are disillusioned: "I didn't know it was going to be like this, and I don't intend to put up with it!" Others of you, a minority, are thinking, *Well, I'm doing okay as it is. But maybe there is something I don't know, a secret that will make my life better.*

Wherever you are in your relationship with the Lord, with your husband, or with the people around you, your needs are unique. Believe me, there *is* a light at the tunnel's end. You say you're different? You say you've tried this "religious bit" before? Your case is too difficult? It's too late? No. "With God *all* things are possible" (Matthew 19:26, emphasis added). That *all* includes you and everything about you, and you can't deny this—that would indict God as a liar, and He cannot lie (Titus 1:2).

"Unless the LORD builds the house, they labor in vain who build it" (Psalm 127:1). Have you been trying, like I was, to build the house by yourself, to do it in your own power? We must come to that point in time when we are willing to admit that *our way* has been wrong or that we are at least willing *to try* His way. This is the first step, recognizing Him as your answer, your source. You go to Him with your life—your bucket of ashes—and you ask, "God, can you make this into something beautiful?"

"Yes," He promises, "but you will have to do it *My way.*"

God's Way

If your concept of God's way is anything like mine was, then what is in reality His way will probably seem foreign to you. I believed in His power, but I felt that it was primarily for the poor, the inept, the oppressed, the weak, and the sick—in other words, for those who were unable to *help themselves.*

I didn't fit into any of those categories. I was strong, or at least I thought I was; and even more important, I wanted others to think I was strong. With clenched teeth, clenched fists, churning stomach, and tears in my eyes, I stubbornly declared time and again, "If I can't do this myself, I'm certainly *not* going to ask God to do it for me!" At other times, in utter despair, I would ask myself, "How many times am I going to have to ask God for help? When am I going to learn to do this on my own?"

This "theology," though I didn't realize it at the time, has a major flaw: The more situations I can master, the more capable I become, the less I will need God. It's the "Lone Ranger" philosophy. My ultimate goal was to advance to that lofty position where I would never need His help at all, to be entirely self-sufficient—or at most, to call on Him only in times of desperate need: "I'm doing okay on my own, God. There are certain areas where I still need You, but I'm working on those! I'll call if I come up against something I can't handle." In other words, "Don't call me; I'll call you."

It sounds all noble and heroic, doesn't it? It wasn't. My world was in a mess because I insisted on doing things *my way*. In fact, it had, for the most part, shut down altogether. And then I discovered God's way.

Every event in our lives, every stimulus and every response, takes place within the following three arenas. If we are to experience the fullness of God's plan for our lives, if we are to *know* Him and His resurrection power, these three arenas must be completely and utterly subjected to and pervaded by Him. This is the foundation of His way.

1. My *self-image:* what I have learned about myself in my world.
2. My *performance:* how I act; how I respond in my world.

3. The *performance of others:* the effect that the people and circumstances in my world have on me.

Self-Image

My self-image was in sad shape: I felt inadequate, clumsy, and unathletic. Nobody likes me, I thought. I'm not any fun, and other people do not enjoy being with me because of my nervous laughter and because I'm generally too quiet (if it's one thing I am not, it's a conversationalist). I wish I were like Doris. She's so quick-witted and has such a great sense of humor.

I have to work hard to be attractive. My nose is coarse looking, my mouth is too big, and I have a space between my front teeth. My upper torso leaves a lot to be desired as far as curves are concerned; my legs are too short, and I have ugly hands.

I hate myself. Oh, how I wish I were different.

My Performance

My performance was bad and getting worse. God Helps Those Who Help Themselves was my motto. (Of course, I couldn't find that anywhere in my Bible to underline and highlight, but I clung to my "self-imposed" theology nevertheless. It gave me a reason—a spiritual, "godly" reason—for my lifestyle.) I've got to do this by myself. I don't want to ask for God's help. He expects me to use the brains He has given me, and I don't want people to think I can't handle this alone . . . so I won't ask anyone to help me.

Besides, the only way I can be sure things are done correctly is for me to do them. I'll work hard, perform perfectly, and then people will accept me and say, "I like Anabel." I will have earned their love.

Performance of Others

The people around me and their performance added to the dilemma of my life. They are the burdens I must bear. They need my advice. I'm a worrier, a peacemaker. I want everyone to be happy, and when someone in my world is hurting or rebellious, it's my responsibility to get in there and straighten things out. The weight is mine.

So where did all this take me? The following is an excerpt from my journal; the date was sometime in the early spring of 1970.

How far I am from being the person God intends for me to be. Never have I been so tempted to give up! I dislike myself—my whole being—so intensely.

I have prayed to be a spiritual wife for such a long time, Lord, and I am not. I don't know what else to do—or not to do. I know You are willing and able, so there must be something in me that blocks Your power. How heartsick I am! Never has my love for my husband been so frail. I am falling more and more into the habit of judging him, of evaluating him, of allowing him to cause me unrest and irritation. I long for someone who I can feel comfortable with—someone in whom I can confide.

I see my complete failure, Lord. How ridiculous it is for me to teach, to counsel, to be looked upon as a godly woman; those who know me best—those who live with me— know what I am, and words become so hollow and meaningless when they see me day after

miserable day, all day long. I will not teach. I
will not have a Bible study. I will not counsel. I
am, basically, an unhappy, unlovely person.
This breaks my heart to confess all this to You,
Lord; I want to blame You. . . . I have asked so
many times to be filled with You and Your
beauty.

These are my feelings. This is the truth. I
am defeated so much of the time, discouraged
and unwilling to allow You to use me. I have
no real friends, no joy, no compassion, no
hope. There is only one positive thing. . . . I
am sorry about my condition.

My self-image was beyond repair; my performance
had ceased to be productive (I no longer felt loved, nor
did I believe I could be worthy of love); and the people
around me were controlling my thoughts and my behavior. These circumstances all funneled into one desire—
into one, final, hopeless escape: self-destruction, suicide.

A.W. Tozer wrote, "Nothing twists and deforms the
soul more than a low or unworthy conception of God."[1]
Our concept of God, our understanding or idea of God,
is of crucial importance. That doesn't mean that we have
to be students of the Bible or that we must be able to
converse on major theological issues. We must simply
search out a clear, true concept of Him and His relationship to us. (*Concept:* that which is conceived in the mind;
a general idea or understanding; a conception.)

This was the root of my problem: how I saw God
and how I believed He saw me—my concept of God and
His ways. I knew what kind of God He was ("Then the
LORD passed by in front of him [Moses] and proclaimed,
'The LORD, the LORD God, compassionate and gracious,

slow to anger, and abounding in lovingkindness and truth . . .' " [Exodus 34:6]), but in the same way I believed I had to earn the love of those around me, I believed I had to earn the love of God.

This isn't God's way; this isn't how He operates. God created us with certain needs, and the greatest and most profound of these needs is our need for love. Deprive someone of love and you deprive them of the very core of life itself. God designed us this way because "God *is* love" (1 John 4:8), and if we had no need for love, we would have no need for God.

I struggled for years to know this love, to achieve and understand it on a personal level. Oh, I knew He loved *us*, but what about *me*, Anabel Gillham? Did He love *me? Could* He love me? And you say, "Anabel, you should have read John 3:16 again: 'For God so loved the world, that He gave His only begotten Son.' " You're right, but that always seemed so all-encompassing and impersonal somehow, as though I were simply one among the millions, an unknown secret admirer with an autographed photo.

God used a very special person in my life to show me how wrong I had been to lump Him in with everyone else, to believe I had to perform in order to "win" or merit His love, thinking that the outline of my way was His outline, too. Mason David Gillham was our second son—profoundly retarded—and it was through my deep love for Mason that God revealed the depths of His love for me.

A Love I Could Comprehend

Mace could sing one song with great gusto, just one: "Jesus Loves Me." He would throw his head back and hold on to that first "Yes" in the chorus just as *long* as he could, and then he would get tickled and almost fall out of his chair. I can still hear him giggle when I think back on those days that seem so distant and so far away. How poignant that memory is to me.

I never doubted for a moment that Jesus loved that profoundly retarded little boy. It didn't matter that he would never sit with the kids in the back of the church and on a certain special night walk down the aisle, take the pastor by the hand, and invite Jesus into his heart. It was entirely irrelevant that he could not quote a single verse of Scripture, that he would never go to high school, or that he would never be a dad. I *knew* that Jesus loved Mason.

What I could *not* comprehend, what I could *not* accept, was that Jesus could love Mason's mother, Anabel. You see, I believed that in order for a person to accept me, to love me, I had to perform for him. My *standard* for getting love was performance-based, so I "performed" constantly, perfectly. In fact, I did not allow anyone to see me when I was not performing perfectly. I never had any close friends because I was convinced that if a person ever *really* got to know me, he wouldn't like me.

I carried this belief into my relationship with God, and, as I began to study the Bible, I found, to my horror, that He knew my every thought, let alone everything I said or did (Psalm 139:1-4). I was standing "bare and wide open to the all-seeing eyes of our living God" (Hebrews 4:13, TLB). What did that mean to me? That meant that He *really knew* me, that He saw me when I wasn't performing well. Based on what I perceived as my responsibility to perform in order to receive acceptance, I concluded without a doubt that He could not possibly love me, that He could never like what He saw.

Mace could never have performed for our love, or for anyone's love, but oh, how we loved him. His condition deteriorated to such a degree—and so rapidly—that we had to institutionalize him when he was very young, so we enrolled him in the Enid State School for Mentally Handicapped Children. We drove regularly the 120 miles to see him, but on this particular weekend, he was at home for a visit. He had been with us since Thursday evening, and it was now Saturday afternoon. As soon as the dinner dishes were done, I would gather his things together and take him back to *his* house. I had done this many times before—and it was never easy—but today God had something in mind that would change my life forever.

As I was washing the dishes, Mason was sitting in his chair watching me, or at least he was looking at me. That's when it began. My emotions were spinning, my stomach started tumbling, and the familiar sickening thoughts of separation and defeat practiced themselves in my mind: *In just a little while, I'm going to start packing Mason's toys and his clothes, and take him away again. I can't do that. I simply cannot do it.* I stopped washing the dishes and got down on my knees in front of Mace. I took his dirty little hands in mine and tried so desperately to reach him.

"Mason, I love you. I love you. If only you could understand how much I love you."

He just stared. He couldn't understand; he didn't comprehend. I stood up and started on the dishes again, but that didn't last long. This sense of urgency—almost a panic—came over me, and once more I dried my hands and knelt in front of my precious little boy.

"My dear Mason, if only you could say to me, 'I love you, Mother.' I *need* that, Mace."

Nothing.

I stood up to the sink again. More dishes, more washing, more crying—and thoughts, foreign to my way of thinking, began filtering into my conscious awareness. I believe God spoke to me that day, and this is what He said: "Anabel, you don't look at your son and turn away in disgust because he's sitting there with saliva drooling out of his mouth; you don't shake your head, repulsed because he has dinner all over his shirt or because he's sitting in a dirty, smelly diaper when he ought to be able to take care of himself. Anabel, you don't reject Mason because all the dreams you had for him have been destroyed. You don't reject him because he doesn't *perform* for you. You love him, Anabel, *just because he is yours.* Mason doesn't willfully reject your love, but you willfully reject Mine. I love you, Anabel, not because you're neat or attractive, not because you do things well, not because you *perform* for Me, but *just because you're Mine.*"

How incredible! How unbelievable! I had struggled for so many years, hating my performance patterns, and yet living to perform, driven to perform, searching out the praise of men and thirsting for the love of God I thought could come only to those who performed well enough to receive it. Yet, God had just shown me that He loved me in spite of anything and everything, and He had shown me in a way that I could understand.

I don't have to do anything for Him; I don't have to *be something* for Him. All I have to do is to accept it: He loves me *just because I am His.* Do you understand? You can know that there is Someone who loves you—not because of the way you look, not because of any talents you might have, not because you're such a hard worker, so efficient and well-organized, not because of your appearance or performance in any way, shape, or form—but because you are His!

* * *

God will not force you to become His, and He will not force you to receive His love, either. It is pure choice, *your* choice. I chose to become His when I was 12 years old. I followed my beloved dad to the altar one Sunday morning and prayed, "Lord, I want You to come into my life. I want You to be real to me and be my God. I accept the gift of Your Son, Jesus, and declare with my heart that I believe in Him."

> But as many as received Him, to them He gave the right to become children of God, even to those who believe in His name (John 1:12).

> If you confess with your mouth Jesus as Lord, and believe in your heart that God raised Him from the dead, you shall be saved (Romans 10:9).

A choice is there for you. Do you see it? You accept . . . or you reject. You say "no," or you say "yes." You *choose* to believe what He has said. You *choose* to receive Him (John 1:12). You *choose* to tell others what you've done (Romans 10:9). And then your life begins to change because of the choices you have made.

You begin to draw from His strength. You cling to His faithfulness to you. You bask in His complete acceptance of you. You retreat into the peace that you find only in His presence. You've come to accept yourself because of Him. You are His . . . and He is yours . . . and you are in love.

After becoming His, there comes what Tozer calls "the glorious pursuit of knowing Him." Anabel . . . in a glorious pursuit! How amazing! How wonderful! But to truly know Him, I had to *acknowledge* His unconditional love, and I had to choose to receive it, to live in it, to believe in it, despite how I felt. I had to choose to give up my way of doing things and allow Him to work His incredible plan in my life, to *become* my life. Ultimately, I had to choose to leave the uncertainty of my world and walk into the certainty of Him.

I went to the altar by myself this time. Dad wasn't there.

3

The Simple Truth

From the onset of my relationship with God, Galatians 2:20 had been one of my favorite verses: "I have been crucified with Christ; and it is no longer I who live, but Christ lives in me; and the life which I now live in the flesh I live by faith in the Son of God, who loved me, and delivered Himself up for me."

I had taught lessons on that verse, and yet I didn't live it. I didn't walk in it! But then, no one had ever taught me how. . .

We enter this world crying for love, for attention—if we aren't crying, a smart slap on the bottom gets us started—and we wind up airing all our grievances: *I don't like it out here! I was warm and now I'm cold. I was all nestled in and cozy, and out here there's nothing but space. The light hurts my eyes, too. It was dark where I came from. Besides all that, I'm hungry!*

So we take this screaming little bundle and try to simulate the womb, to settle him down and make him all comfy again. We put him in a dry diaper and a footie gown; we wrap him in a soft, warm receiving blanket and put him in a bassinet, just his size; then we put a bottle in his mouth, and he stops crying—for a while anyway. Then he starts again. What is he crying for? Love. To be held. To receive the positive touch of humanity. Closeness. Security.

When asked what caused him to focus his years of research on love and just what it means to mankind, Dr. Martin Bergmann, professor of psychology at New York University, credited the observations of other psychologists who found that some babies in foundling hospitals—provided with good care but no love—died. "Babies *cannot live* without love," Bergmann said. "Older people do better, but they never do very well."[1] Certain little ones will decide just to quit trying, and they don't cry anymore. They close their tearless eyes and hurry back to their creator.

Well, *we* didn't die, but that doesn't mean that our need for love was satisfied. Some of us were held close, touched, and cooed to. Our dads sang lullabies; our grandparents vied for our affections. There was no doubt that *we* were loved. But for others of us, the people in our world didn't hear what we were saying, or they didn't care. They blatantly neglected or carelessly ignored us. They even became irritated by our demands and reacted in cruel ways, doing things that let us know they were *not* going to allow us to control them and were *not* interested in satisfying our need for love. Rejection.

The curtain nevertheless had been drawn on our magnificent search. We were on stage, so we set out to explore our world, to find out what had to be done in order to be loved and accepted. For those of us who found something that worked, we programmed it into our computer (brain) and used it over and over again to get people to love and accept us. In other words, we developed techniques for getting love, or we developed techniques for coping with *not* getting love. These patterns, along with all the other self-generated methods we use to meet our needs, fall under the classification called "flesh" in the Bible (Paul talks about *his* flesh in his letter to the Philippians—3:3-6).

Flesh: Your ability (or inability) to satisfy your human, God-given needs in your own way, using your strength and your resources apart from Christ.

Flesh: When you were a little child, no one ever said to you, "I love you." There was never any touching or tenderness. Closeness was not communicated. Because of this, you may have developed a pattern for feeling insecure, unloved, and unlovely: *After all, if no one loves me, then I must be an unlovable person. There's something wrong with me.* Your unique flesh patterns were built.

Flesh: A little girl is designed by God to need her daddy to touch her, hold her, talk to her, spend time with only her! She learns about males this way, how to interact with them. But your dad was gone all the time. Or you were raised by a single mom. Now, as a woman, you may be very insecure in male relationships, so you shy away from them. If a "comfortable" male friend begins to drop hints he might want to deepen the relationship, you get panicky. You're scared. You want it, and yet you don't. To the other extreme, you may crave this male attention, and you have allowed this craving to control you . . . sexual promiscuity, a lot of boyfriends, intimate fantasies about men. Your unique flesh patterns were formed.

Flesh: You discovered very early in life that the people you lived with, Mom and Dad, would "give you strokes" (love you) if you did something really well—if your report card sported all "A's"; if the kitchen was super clean; if your room was well-organized. Anything worth doing was worth doing really *well*. Today? You may be a driven person who has to be "doing" something all the time and who critically evaluates her every accomplishment to be sure it is done "really *well*." Or you may have given up and don't give a rip what anything looks like. Your unique flesh patterns were carefully constructed.

We are all seeking love, and, as we saw in the previous chapter, God created us with this need for love in hopes that we would turn to Him to have that need met, in hopes that we would realize that only He, and no one else, can fill that void. When we allow *Him* to meet that need, we are doing what Paul called "walking in the Spirit"; but when we continue to use those techniques we developed *apart* from Him, we are walking "after the flesh" (Romans 8:4-6).

I don't know what your flesh patterns are, but I do know what mine are—and I know Bill's, too. I learned to perform and to perform well, remember? People loved me when I did. I came out *strong*, with what Bill calls USDA-choice flesh, or flesh that works. Bill, in an effort to maintain and bolster *his* self-acceptance, developed a pattern for being threatened by strong females (and that was Anabel, bless her heart). He had one way to deal with these obnoxious creatures—*destroy them.*

Did I realize that when I married Him? No. Did Bill

realize that my strength and perfectionism would cause him to try to destroy me? No. We had not yet experienced a "close encounter" with our unique flesh patterns; we hadn't put our toothbrushes in the same glass, had one closet, or started using the same electrical outlets.

The flesh patterns I had developed combined with the marriage I was in eventually brought me to my knees. I met my Waterloo, my decisive defeat. What is your Waterloo? A divorce? Success that has eluded you? A relationship with another family member? A chemical dependency? An illusive dream? An abusive marriage? A rebellious child? And because of what has happened in your life, you have finally concluded that your flesh patterns just won't work any longer. What has brought you to your knees? What has caused you to say, "Lord, I can't"?

He *can*. No matter what the circumstances are. No matter what the flesh patterns are. The change He brought in my life bears this out! So while I talk about my marriage and the events that were unique to my situation, be thinking of your own Waterloo. My dear sister, God will meet you there on that ravaged battleground.

How Did This Happen to Me?

As I share with you about our marriage, it will seem as though Bill was the vicious villain. Not really. He wasn't the only bad guy—he was a hurting man, a threatened male fighting to survive in the ring with a superstrong female, a perfectionistic performer who could do anything he could do, and better. Our marriage was not a "mutual admiration society"; it was a "mutual extermination society." We were destroying each other.

I went into marriage with some positive attributes. I

was an efficient, outgoing, self-confident person with impressive records. My technique, or flesh pattern, for getting acceptance and love had been successful—performing, in all ways, performing. After walking in performance-based acceptance for years, one generally evolves into performance-based *self-acceptance*. If that person is a *super*performer as I was, then nine times out of ten she is also a *super*perfectionist who is *super*sensitive to any kind of criticism: "Don't tell me that I did it wrong; I did not do it wrong. I did it perfectly. In fact, I stayed up past midnight working on it just to be sure it was done perfectly." A superperformer (Anabel) demands perfect performance out of herself. Bill did not demand perfect performance out of himself; rather, he demanded it out of the people around him, the people who were to meet his needs.

A performer is driven to achieve, and though I was discouraged when I didn't do well during my school years, there was always another tomorrow, another chance, another place, another contest. But for me, marriage was the big one! This was it! You only get one chance, and I wasn't winning. Every time I forged into the lead, Bill would trip me. I would get up, lick my wounds, brush myself off, and start running again. But I was being torn down, and to top it all, I couldn't get out of this "contest" and enter another one.

In school I had learned to protect my image by never having any close friends; I didn't want anyone to see me when I was not "up" and performing well (better to stay home and miss the party than to go and not be Miss Popularity). You see, my mind-set was that people would not accept me or like me if I didn't perform well enough to please them, and in my marriage, that mindset had been validated. Bill *knew* me. He lived with me and saw me when I was not performing at my best, and because *he* didn't like me, my fears were confirmed: *You get to know me and you won't like me.*

I was running into big problems. The technique for getting love that I had so carefully constructed and maintained for 22 years was no longer working.

It was during my years in college and while dating Bill that I first came to know depression. But Bill was my savior! All I needed to do was call him and say, "Honey, I need you," and he would come. A walk through the campus, a trip to the Do-Nut-Hole, an hour or so in the parlor of the dorm, and everything was okay again. He was simply Mr. Wonderful—perhaps that's why I didn't pray about marrying him. Surely after being constant companions for five years, you *know* someone, don't you? I knew Bill; that is, I *thought* I knew Bill. He was thoughtful, considerate, and kind. Never could I have asked for anyone to meet my needs more completely. He was my "knight in shining armor" come valiantly to do my bidding—to shelter me, to encourage me, to protect me.

And then (sigh) we got married. When he got me into the castle with the drawbridge up, my knight tarnished almost beyond recognition. My attentive, thoughtful, considerate, loving hero became inconsiderate, unkind, profane, vulgar, and, worst of all, critical; his sarcastic tongue dripped with venom.

The most horrible change was in the way he talked to me, the things he said to me. I couldn't do *anything* right. I never shall forget that one Saturday morning in our first honeymoon apartment. Bill said, "Honey, I'd like to talk to you for a moment." He took me by the hand and led me into our living room. We sat down on the little flowered settee (which I had just finished recovering), and he said to me, softly, "Honey, I wish you would learn to do at least *one thing* well."

I thought I was doing "well," but obviously I wasn't. How did I know? Because Bill said so. But if he expected this to destroy me (remember that his game plan was to destroy strong, capable women who threatened his male role), then his expectations were wrong. His criticism motivated me to do bigger and better and more perfect things. You see, I was performing for Bill, trying to get him to praise me. I craved it. It was my only ticket to self-acceptance, to acceptance period! I'd been living on praise for most of my 22 years; it was my lifeblood. If I didn't get it, I wouldn't make it. So I was engaged in a life-or-death battle with Bill, and I was losing. Oh, but I was strong and determined to fight!

For instance, when Bill moonlighted in the oil fields during his summer respite from teaching, he would leave the house at 7:30 A.M. and come home in the evening, dirty, tired, hungry, and in a bad mood. My thinking? *What can I do for Bill today to please him? I know. I'll mow the lawn, edge everything, prune the hedges, and rake it all up. Then when he comes home, he'll say, "Would you look at this lawn? Talk about manicured! Did you do this all by yourself, Honey? Looks great."* (Surely he will notice and praise me? No.)

But I didn't give up. I was a performer, right? You must understand, I spelled love, p-r-a-i-s-e. I was starving for praise. *Let me see. Tomorrow, I know what I'll do. I'll have a freezer of his favorite ice cream sitting on the porch, and when he sees it he'll say, "Wow! I can't think of anything that would please me more right now than a dish of home-made, vanilla ice cream."* (He *will* say something like that, won't he? No.)

Bill's plan wasn't working either. I was still coming on as strong, if not stronger, as always, and that threatened him all the more. So he switched to Plan B—a more destructive plan. He began pointing out things I could not possibly change. On one occasion we were going to a square dance, and I, of course, looked perfect (performers always look perfect—they don't leave the house until they do). Bill looked over at me, all dressed up in my frilly square-dance dress, and said, "You know, I can't imagine anyone wanting to dance with you." Needless to say, the evening lost its glamour.

I remember another time, walking out the door for an evening with friends, when Bill turned and casually said, "Honey, try not to laugh so much tonight. You make people uncomfortable when you do that." He was playing a game called, "Let's Destroy Anabel." He was fighting for survival, and so the one who had been my deliverer *from* the threat of depression during college suddenly became the reason *for* my depression—and it wouldn't go away. I was living with it.

My personality began to change. From valedictorian and campus sweetheart—from being efficient, competent, capable, and outgoing—I became defeated, insecure, and doubted my ability to carry out the most simple task. My hands moved so slowly folding clothes that I wondered if I would *ever* get them all done. Bill's hateful, caustic remarks had succeeded in destroying my self-image. Me, pretty? Me, desirable? Me, capable?

Do you understand that I was building *new* patterns? That because of the circumstances in my private world, I was fighting for survival? My performance, my perfectionism, my ability to do things well—that "flesh" that had proven so effective over the years—none of that mattered anymore.

Bill's survival techniques proved to be effective. My techniques just wouldn't work any longer. Other people might have praised me; others might have given me awards or prizes or applause. But I needed that praise from the one person I had chosen out of the whole world to be my lover, my confidant, and my friend—I needed it from Bill.

After seven, long years of marriage, Bill became a Christian. He had somehow come to realize, after all that time, the person he had become, and he called out to God. God heard him, knew the sincerity of his heart, and responded to his cry of repentance. That man is no more, but his changing was not an overnight miracle—the horrible sarcastic tongue remained.

Twenty years into the marriage I still had not given up. But by that time I had developed and perfected a new pattern: depression. Deep depression. A coping mechanism for living in my miserable private world. I couldn't remember anything nice happening the day before, and there was no hope that something nice would happen the next day. I had only "today," and I had learned from the man I lived with that I did not perform well on "todays." So I wanted out, and the only acceptable "out" for this performer was suicide. That way I wouldn't have to face people after my poor performance.

Throughout the desperate extremes of this entire crisis situation, I never turned away from God. I was going to church regularly. I read my Bible. I prayed. I recall sleepless nights, pacing the floor, sobbing, and calling out, "My God! This man is destroying me! What can I do?" *But I never gave God a chance. I kept trying to do it all myself.* I was trying to cart the horse! I had invested in a good pair of leather gloves so I wouldn't get calluses rolling rocks. I had planted a carrot garden and carried an extra "tongue wheel" in the cart at all times. Very efficient. "Tomorrow," I would say. "Another day. A new start." And then I would sit down, make my plans, and write out a list of new resolutions.

Giving Up

New starts. New resolutions. I've gone through quite a few of both. Have you ever told yourself, "Another day. I'm going to do better today than I did yesterday. I simply must!" Or have you written down all the desires of your heart and promised yourself, "I am going to do these things. I *can* do it!"

But new starts and resolutions are not what God had in mind. It was the crucial realization that I *can't* do it, that awareness of my complete incapability to do one single thing—that's what He wanted. Complete dependency on Him. For the perfectionist, for that self-made person, for that strong, capable, efficient woman whose independence had been so carefully programmed—for Anabel—that was a terribly difficult truth to accept.

I still remember the night my stubborn, independent, strong-willed self came to that realization. I had gone to bed. It had been a bad day. I don't remember why—I had a lot of bad days. I was sobbing, praying, "God, I don't understand what is going on in my life. My marriage is so far away from what I long for it to be; my kids are not turning out the way I want them to. And I'm so tired. I've given, given, and given, and I don't think I can give anymore. I have made one grand mess of everything."

Then I said what I had never said in all my 40-some-odd years of life: "I give up. I have failed. *I can't do it*. If anything is going to come out of this marriage and these kids, if anything is going to come out of this life, You're going to have to do it, because I can't."

Do you have any idea how difficult it was for me to say those words? I had a collection of well-rehearsed, standard answers: "I think I can. . . . Yes, I'll be glad to do that for you. . . . I'll certainly try. . . . Well, it isn't my forte, but I'll give it a shot. . . ." To admit defeat was as incomprehensible, as un-American, as "the little engine that could" giving up. Not then, though. My strength was gone. I was broken.

I believe God spoke to me that night in the quiet of my bedroom. A thought came into my conscious aware-ness that was foreign to my way of thinking. It was a simple little phrase: "Thank you, Anabel. I will do it all *for* you."

That was the beginning, and I do mean the *begin-ning*. A tiny seed of understanding had been planted; I was awakening into the morning of *His* way: *Jesus Christ (the only one who ever lived the Christian life) came into me because He wants to live His life, the Christian life, through me.* It's that simple. Oh, it wasn't the birth of this truth in my life; it had been mine ever since I was 12 years old when I accepted Christ as my Savior. But it had been lying dormant for 30 years. I didn't even know it was there.

That night, though, I needed that truth and was ready to use what had been tucked away for so long. My I-can-handle-it routine had brought me through a lot of deep waters, but God ultimately had to allow me to get so far out and sink so deep—without even a board to cling to—that I had to confess, both to Him and to myself, *"I can't handle it any longer."* He had been waiting for me to say that ever since He, through my invitation and by my permission, had come to dwell within me.

From Adam to Jesus

From the onset of my relationship with God, Galatians 2:20, which encompasses this principle of Christ's life through the believer, had been one of my favorite verses: "I have been crucified with Christ; and it is no longer I who live, but Christ lives in me; and the life which I now live in the flesh I live by faith in the Son of God, who loved me, and delivered Himself up for me." I had taught lessons on that verse, and yet I didn't live it. I didn't walk in it! But then, no one had ever taught me how.

When did that "crucifixion" take place in my life?

When Jesus was crucified (Romans 6:6; Galatians 2:20).

But how could that be? I wasn't even born yet!

Let me try to explain. Just as our physical characteristics were determined at birth by our biological parents, our spiritual characteristics were determined at birth by our spiritual father, the "prince of the power of the air," Satan (Ephesians 2:1,2). You did not *become* a sinner, a spirit-son of Satan; you were *born* a sinner because you were born *in Adam* (Romans 5:11-19). *Birth determines identity.* You were born hostile and alienated from God (Colossians 1:21), a child of wrath (Ephesians 2:3), condemned (Romans 6:23), spiritually dead (Ephesians 2:1,5), an enemy of God (Romans 5:8-10), and a slave of sin (Romans 6:17).

But when you invited Jesus into your life, you were reborn (1 Peter 1:23). *You were transferred out of Satan's kingdom (Adam's lineage) and into God's kingdom (Jesus' lineage; see Colossians 1:13).* You've been transferred from Florida to Oregon. You can't live in both places at the same time!

Christ is now your spiritual progenitor. You have experienced a new birth. You are now a part of God's family. And just as you had all of Adam's spiritual characteristics when you were in his life, you now have all of Christ's spiritual characteristics because you are in *His* life. Your death, burial, and resurrection with Him—your new life, your new nature in Him—this is His provision for life. Not just eternal life, but your life today! This is His provision for your transformation. *Your identity has changed!* Today. Right now.

> *Therefore, just as through one man [Adam] sin entered into the world, and death through sin, and so death spread to all men, because all sinned. . . . For if by the transgression of the one [Adam], death reigned through the one, much more those who receive the abundance of grace and of the gift of righteousness will reign in life through the One, Jesus Christ. So then as through one transgression there resulted condemnation to all men, even so through one act of righteousness [Jesus' death and resurrection] there resulted justification of life to all men. For as through the one man's disobedience the many were made sinners, even so through the obedience of the One the many will be made righteous* (Romans 5:12,17-19).

When you are "in Christ" (have invited Him into your heart), your whole history changes. You were crucified with Him (Galatians 2:20), buried with Him (Romans 6:4), and raised a brand-new person (2 Corinthians 5:17); Christ is now your life (Colossians 3:4); you have the Holy Spirit living in you (1 Corinthians 6:19); you are a partaker of His divine nature (2 Peter

1:4); you are holy and blameless before Him (Ephesians 1:4); you are seated with Him in heaven (Ephesians 2:6); and you are loved (John 16:27). Incredible!

A Woman's Choice

Years ago I was chairman of the prayer committee for the big, county-wide meeting that was coming to Durant. We had planned an all-night prayer vigil for Saturday, and the schedule was almost filled. I had chosen the midnight hour, and there was only one slot left—5 A.M. I took that one, too. I didn't want the chain to be broken.

We were meeting at the Lutheran Church just half a block from our house on Main Street, so Bill felt safe in letting me walk the distance alone. (How times have changed!) Even though I made a gallant effort, I dozed through most of the midnight watch, but I was "bright-eyed and bushy-tailed" when five rolled around—early morning is one of my favorite times of day.

Oh, I know, I was supposed to be praying for the minister and all the people, but I was having a rough time (per usual), so I included Anabel in my conversation. As I prayed, I said something like this: "Lord, I don't completely understand Galatians 2:20, 'I have been crucified with Christ and I no longer live, but Christ lives in me,' but I want to claim this truth. Please help me." And since I was all alone in that little chapel, I stretched out on the floor in a "crucified" pose and told God, "I accept this from You, today, for my life."

I made a choice—with my mind, with my will—and it is *your* choice as well:

> Lord, I've done it my way for so long; I
> don't understand Galatians 2:20 and all that it

means for me, but I want to claim its truth for my life. You say that You now indwell me in the presence of the Holy Spirit; You say that I have been crucified, buried, and raised with You, and that the only One who ever lived the Christian life, You, promised to live that same life through me. By faith I receive what You have said in Your Word and believe it. From opening my eyes in the morning to the most stressful part of my day, I thank You that You will do it *all* for me, through me.

When I made that choice, my life didn't change overnight. I simply began to be consciously aware of my actions and my thoughts; I began choosing His Way, trusting Him to be my strength, my power, my wisdom—*my very life*—saying no to thoughts that were contrary to what I knew was truth—and holding tenaciously to that truth.

I'm still doing the very same thing today, and I made that choice almost 20 years ago. Step by sometimes painful step, I have learned and am learning to allow Him to express *His* life through me, as a woman, as the wife of Bill Gillham and the mother of my sons, whether I am lecturing, making a banana-cream pie, digging in the marigolds, or cleaning the commode.

Jesus wants desperately to do the same thing for you. And He will. He will live His life through you. He will do it *all* for you—over and over and over again. . . .

Personal Reflections

Look up each of the Scriptures and on a separate sheet of paper write down the phrase that describes your spiritual characteristics as you were "in" Adam.

Date of My Physical Birth: _____

Because I was born in Adam, I received the following spiritual characteristics from my *spiritual father,* *Satan:*

Matthew 18:11	Romans 6:23
John 8:38	Romans 8:2
John 8:41	2 Corinthians 4:4
John 8:44	Ephesians 2:1
Romans 5:8	Ephesians 2:3
Romans 5:10	Ephesians 5:6
Romans 6:17	Ephesians 5:8
Romans 6:19	Colossians 1:21

These spiritual characteristics became mine, through my spiritual progenitor, Adam, when I was physically born.

Date of My Birth into God's Family: _____

However, they ceased to be my spiritual characteristics when I accepted Christ, dying with Him, being reborn into the family of God, and claiming Christ as my spiritual progenitor. I accepted Jesus Christ and was born into God's family.

The following spiritual characteristics became mine when I was born from above into God's family, when I accepted Jesus Christ as my Savior and Lord. Colossians 1:13: "He delivered us from the domain of darkness, and transferred us to the kingdom of His beloved Son." (Add the key phrases from the following verses to your paper.)

Ezekiel 36:26,27	2 Corinthians 5:21
Romans 6:4	Galatians 2:20

Romans 8:1	Ephesians 2:5
Romans 11:16	Ephesians 2:6
1 Corinthians 2:16	Ephesians 2:19
1 Corinthians 6:11	Colossians 2:10
1 Corinthians 6:19	Colossians 3:3
2 Corinthians 2:14	Colossians 3:4
2 Corinthians 2:15	2 Peter 1:4
2 Corinthians 5:17	1 John 4:10

This is who I am now *in Christ Jesus*. I confirm this and choose to walk in my true identity from this day forward.

Signature: _____ Date: _____

Jesus Christ Comes to Dwell in Me

As a new creation, Jesus Christ comes to dwell in me! (Look up each verse and note what it says about you.)

John 14:15-17	Ephesians 2:22
John 14:23	Ephesians 3:16-21
Romans 8:9-11	1 Thessalonians 4:8
1 Corinthians 3:16,17	2 Timothy 1:14
1 Corinthians 6:19	James 4:5
2 Corinthians 6:16	1 John 2:27
2 Corinthians 13:5	1 John 3:24
Galatians 2:20	1 John 4:13
Galatians 4:6	1 John 4:15

I, _____, accept this as *truth* for my life this _____ day of _____, _____. Thank You, dear Lord Jesus, for living *in* me and meeting life *through* me every moment of every day.

Reprogramming Your Personal Computer

Reprogramming your computer will mean the difference between days of despair and days of peace and confidence, the difference between relationships that have simply existed for years and ones that exude the love of Christ. It will mean walking in obedience and allowing Christ to be your life. And it will mean coming to know that life at its fullest.

Is it possible that this might be the key to living?

She was a small woman, but her chin gave her away. It said, "I'm determined, and I don't give up easily." The door had barely closed behind her when she started crying. "Anabel, I can't do anything right. I'm not a good mother, I'm not a good wife, I can't even work in the garden and do it well!"

I began talking to her, searching behind the faded freckles and matronly facade for the walls and fences I knew were there. . . .

"Yes, Anabel, my mom loved me."

"How do you know she loved you, Gail?"

"Because she took care of me, I suppose. She made my dresses. She cooked for me and washed my clothes. Yes, she loved me."

"Did she ever tell you that she loved you?"

"Oh . . . well, not really. She was a very private person."

"How about your dad? What was your relationship like with him?"

"Okay, I guess. Dad had a favorite saying about me."

"What was it?"

"I guess if he said it once, he said it a million times: 'If you ever want anything done right, don't ask Gail to do it.'"

I'm so glad Gail was determined. . . .

Understanding Why We Do What We Do

I've talked with many women who are struggling to meet the demands of their everyday existence. In these one-on-one encounters, I look for the answers to these two questions: (1) How willing are you to abandon the past? and (2) How willing are you to give up *your* way for *His* way?

I've shared with you how I discovered God's way. It wasn't exactly an exciting treasure hunt! I played out my way as far as it would go, and, when I found myself stranded and in complete desperation, I told God that if anything was going to come of my life He would have to do it (you could hardly call that first-prize performance). I gave up, and do you remember how He responded? "Thank you, Anabel. I will do it all for you."

This is God's way—*allowing Him to express His life through us.* If we are ever to live above our circumstances—despite our circumstances—then we must not only be willing to submit to His ways, but we must also, more often than not, be willing to abandon our past. And that's what we'll be talking about in this chapter.

For the most part, you are what your environment throughout the formative years of your life fashioned you to be, or perhaps *forced* you to be. By "environment," I am referring to what happened to you in your early, private world—that world of people around you and their interaction with you. These crucial, early years of life greatly determine the blueprints of your personality: how and what you think of yourself; how you deal with stress; how you interact with others; and your ability to give love, to receive love, or to exist without love.

Was your world traumatic and chaotic? Or was it peaceful? Were you surrounded by hostility, anger, and hate? Or were you enveloped in love and patience? Did fear and insecurity hold you in their viselike grip every day? When you closed your eyes at night, were you still crying from the abuse and rejection? Or were there pleasant memories of laughter and touching?

Gail had never *known* love. A child cannot think abstract thoughts and logically deduce, "Mother is simply a private person and expresses her love by cooking dinner for me." No, only concrete communication gets through to a child: eye contact, touching, words and the inflection of those words, time, body language, etc.

"I love you."

"You're special."

"Come sit on my lap and we'll read a story."

"You're learning to do things so well."

"Will you hold my hand?"

"I like to do things with you. You're fun."

"God gave me such a nice present when He gave you to me."

"Be sure to give me a good-night kiss when you come in."

Gail had experienced commitment from her mother, not love. Commitment is an integral part of parenting, but commitment without expressed love can be sterile, cold, and harsh. It leaves a void where love should have been planted, tended, and perfected. Gail also had been rejected and ridiculed by the most important man in her life, her dad. All she wanted from either of them, all she desperately *needed,* was their love and acceptance.

Where had Gail learned that she "can't do anything right"? From her dad, years ago. He told her so a million times—or so it seemed to her young, formative mind—and it was burned into her memory banks. She grew to *believe* that she couldn't do *one thing* right, and that if you asked her to do anything, you should expect failure. Add to this her belief that she is an unlovely, unlovable person (which her "very private" mother never contradicted and, through her silence, confirmed), and you have an adult who is emotionally insecure in her self-image and in her ability to perform.

To see how Gail came to believe and feel this way, we must first draw a simple, biblical picture of man. The Bible teaches that every person is made up of three integrated parts: *spirit, soul,* and *body* (1 Thessalonians 5:23) (see Figure 4.1).

Every person is made up of three integrated parts:
spirit, soul, and body (1 Thessalonians 5:23).

Figure 4.1

Most of us have never really thought about the soul. The word *soul* and the word *psychology* come from the same root word, meaning *personality*. Your *soul* is your personality—your mind, will, and emotions (see Figure 4.2). Your *body* is simply the vehicle through which your soul—the real you—communicates with and relates to people. It's what *you* are housed in during your stay on earth; if you didn't have a "live" body, you couldn't interact with people.

Your soul is your personality, or your mind, your will,
and your emotions.

Figure 4.2

In the same way, your *spirit* is the vehicle through which you—your soul—communicates with and relates to God, and if you don't have a live spirit, you can't interact with Him. So when you are born physically, you are given the capacity to interact with the world around you, and when you are "born again"—spiritually born—you are given the capacity to interact with God (see Figure 4.3).

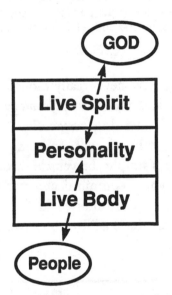

Your body is the vehicle through which your soul (the real you) communicates with and relates to people.

When you are "born again" (spiritually born), you are given the capacity to interact with God.

Figure 4.3

How Flesh Patterns Are Formed

Gail had a live spirit (she had chosen God's way and invited Jesus to come into her life); she was a "new creature in Christ" (2 Corinthians 5:17). But why did she feel unloved, inadequate, insecure, and rejected? Why did she believe that she was worthless and couldn't do anything right? How did she come to be this way?

Like Gail, you have a mind and you have emotions. Your *brain*, or computer as I like to call it, is part of your body; it's a body organ like your liver, right? Your *mind*, on the other hand, is the seat of your personality, or soul; your brain and your mind are not the same (see Figure 4.4). Your mind uses your brain as you would use a personal computer. Your emotions respond to whatever you choose—with your will—to set your mind on.

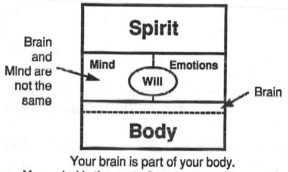

Your brain is part of your body.
Your mind is the seat of your personality or soul.

Figure 4.4

For example, if you *believe* there's a burglar in the house, you'll *feel* like there's a burglar in the house—muscles tensed, alert to the slightest sound, eyes wide and focused on the darkness, pulse rate climbing, and all the while trying to remember where the flashlight is. That isn't difficult for us to understand.

In the same way, if you *believe* you're a loser—and it *is* a choice—you'll *feel* like a loser: You'll hesitate to go to the party; you'll sit by yourself in church; you'll consider yourself worthless as an employee; you'll doubt that your husband or children love you; you'll hate to shop and spend money on yourself; you'll constantly degrade yourself and your performance; you'll be unable to receive gifts or help from friends when you're flat on your back; and on it goes. The theme of your thought-life will be, *Why should anyone care for me? I'm such a loser.*

Let's say a spider comes to visit you while you're in bed some night. He can crawl around on your pillow, creep across the sheets, and even tunnel through your hair, yet you won't be aware of that forward visitor. But let his little hairy legs touch your face, and you'll be "aware" of him all right! Within the second after he touches your cheek, you perceive him, your brain processes the input, your mind concludes that *something hairy and little touched my face*, your emotions rocket to the top, and your will chooses to act. That's when the arms flail, the covers fly, you hit the light switch, and the hunt is on!

Now, after you've sent the spider to spider heaven, your mind realizes that the threat is over and *instantly* relaxes. You *know* the culprit has been taken care of, right? (You picked it up in a tissue, twisted it real good, threw it in the toilet, and watched to be sure it flushed!) But how about your emotions? On a scale of one to ten, they've been hitting an 11! And even after you know the spider is no more, your emotions dilly-dally around on level ten for 15 minutes, gradually come down to eight, and then lodge on seven for an hour. You may not get back to sleep for another 45 minutes, and that's in spite of your knowing everything is okay!

Let me ask you a question: What if you *live* with a

"spider"? What if you *grew up* with a spider? Your mother, maybe, or your dad. What if every day the spider touches your cheek four, five, 20 times? Where will your emotions be? On eight most of the time. And because of this, they will probably get *stuck* in the upper part of the scale because they are there so much, if not all, of the time. *You won't even know what it's like to be at a five on your emotional scale, much less at one.* And you will say things like: "I cry easily," "I have a short fuse," "I don't handle emotional things very well." Or you may have put your emotions in a locked box that no one is ever allowed to open.

Because no one ever told Gail anything to the contrary, she not only *believed* she was a born loser, she *felt* like a born loser (remember that your emotions are going to respond to what your mind is set on). Her mind had been programmed—"a million times or more"—and as a result, her emotions just couldn't find their way back to the starting point. Her feelings were stuck on LOSER. That's why the door had barely closed behind her when she started crying.

Gail's emotions were at the top; they were high all the time. Whenever some small, emotionally stressful situation came along, she didn't have the flexibility on her emotional scale to tolerate it. She would break. And what do you suppose patterns like this will bring about in a marriage relationship? Or in any close relationship—roommates, teacher/pupil, mother/daughter, boss/employee, coworkers, friends?

So how do *your* "blueprints" look? What are your "habit patterns"? What do you believe about yourself, and where are your emotions?

Whatever or wherever they are, don't blame your parents. They were children, too, complete with formative years. They, too, learned about themselves from the people around them and are who they are today because of, or in spite of, their early home environment, because of what happened to them in their own private world. All they asked was to be loved—just like you, just like me.

The real question isn't, what did other people do to you? but rather, how did you respond? What walls did you build?

A Lifetime of Walls

She was 88 years old—a delightful person. She chatted about everything with great enthusiasm—her children, her husband, their lives, and their plans. "They're all doing so well," she said.

I listened and asked questions, letting her know I was interested in her life. Eventually, the superficial "small talk" ebbed, and we went below the surface. She began to weep softly.

"I've never shared with anyone but the children what happened that morning. . . .

"Papa never showed me any love. He just didn't talk to me. He was quite a baseball fan. . . . Mamma was the same way, but then, she had so many responsibilities. I never really knew her. She didn't have time for me. . . .

"My son told me that he hated me, and then he left and stayed away from home for 12 years. . . ."

Such a carefully built wall, and no one had been behind it for more than 70 years.

A Question of Identity

We build walls and live behind them. Walls of self-protection: "I refuse to be hurt again." Walls of deception: "No one will ever know. No one cares. Why share my hurt?" Walls of guilt: "Oh! If only I could have that one hour to live over again!" Walls of behavior: "I'll get my way! They'll be sorry!" Emotional walls: "I cannot say, 'I love you.'"

These are the patterns we erect in our private world, unique because of our environment and the circumstances that have come into our lives.

The foundation for my carefully constructed walls was performance-based acceptance. Many of you, I'm sure, are members of POA, Inc. (Performers of America). It permeates our culture. You can build varying patterns on the foundation of performance-based acceptance, and yours may be entirely different from mine. I was controlled by perfectionism, extreme sensitivity, thoughts of inferiority, and constant introspection. I was always evaluating my performance, and because I *believed* I was inferior, because I *felt* inferior, my evaluation was always charted on the negative end of the graph.

When I married a man who did not accept me (my performance wasn't paying off) and would not praise me (praise is the "lifeblood" of a performer), I developed some new patterns: depression, mood swings, tears, pouting, self-hatred, and suicidal tendencies. What a mess!

And this is now me, this is *just the way I am,* right? Meet Anabel Gillham. These are the habit patterns, complete with correlating emotions, that have been deeply ingrained into me. This is who I am today, and this is who I will be until the day I die. I have to live with it, and you have to put up with it (sigh).

Now wait just a minute! *That's not true!* According to the Scriptures, that old Anabel died in Christ (Galatians 2:20), and I was reborn "not of blood, nor of the will of the flesh, nor of the will of man, but of God"

(John 1:13). I became *someone new* when I was born again (2 Corinthians 5:17), and the life of Christ became my life (Colossians 3:4). Furthermore, I was transferred out of the kingdom of darkness and into the kingdom of light (Ephesians 5:8; Colossians 1:13). I'm different! I'm new! And as this new creation in Christ, these old patterns of how I think, how I act, and how I feel that I have walked in for years *are no longer me* (see Figure 4.5).

But then why are you still depressed at times, Anabel? Why do you still feel, sometimes, that your performance dictates your acceptance?

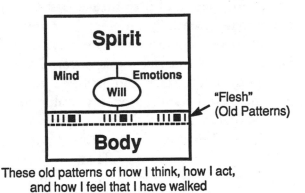

These old patterns of how I think, how I act,
and how I feel that I have walked
in for years are no longer me!

Figure 4.5

We're back to those "old ways" again. Yes, those patterns were indelibly burned into my memory banks; yes, they controlled me; yes, they are still deposited in my brain; and yes, they still influence my behavior. But now they are simply my version of the flesh (see Figure 4.6). What we have here is a question of identity: *Who* I am and *what* I am versus how I *feel* and how I sometimes *act*.

As we saw in the last chapter, I am a new person.

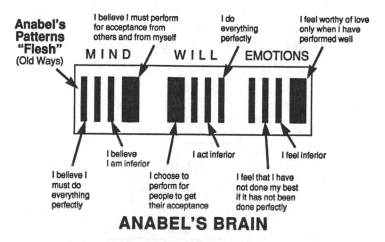

ANABEL'S BRAIN

An enlarged view showing some of the
patterns burned into my brain through the years.
The heavier lines denote deep patterns.

Figure 4.6

And I'm not a sinner saved by grace either. That is as
incomprehensible as being a "married single." I can't be
married and single at the same time, and in the same way
I can't be a sinner and a saint simultaneously. Granted, I
still sin, but I'm not a *sinner*—I am a *saint* who sins, a
saint who deplores her sinful behavior. Once I was a sinner, but when Christ saved me, I became a saint. (Have
you noticed that Paul opens the majority of his letters by
addressing the church members as "saints"?)

My identity has changed, and those old patterns are
now my *old ways,* my flesh. In computer language, they
are "programs" in my computer (my brain) burned into
my memory banks. And though they will continue to
manifest themselves in my behavior and in my emotions,
they *do not* determine my identity. Birth determines identity, and I have been reborn (see Figure 4.7).

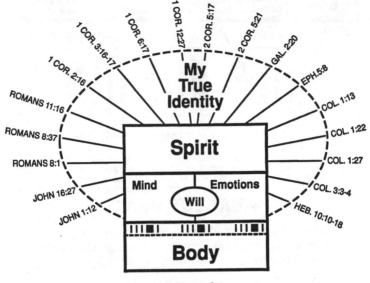

Figure 4.7

These old ways are habits, and habits don't vanish overnight. Though you are new, you may still choose (with your will) to allow those old habit patterns to control you. In other words, you can still choose to sin (we'll see how and why in the next chapter). These patterns are broken and reversed only by recognizing them for what they are, and then by reprogramming our computers on a moment-by-moment basis and over a good deal of time ("Be transformed by the renewing of your mind" [Romans 12:2]). Now go back and read this section again.

What We Believe to Be True

Do you know how important it is that you understand what I have just shared with you? You *must realize* that regardless of what your background is like, regardless

of what you have been told and retold again and again—
"if he said it once, he said it a million times"—regardless
of how you *feel*, what you have done, how you act, or
what you think of yourself, you are a *new and different
person* now that you are *in* Christ Jesus, now that you
have asked Him into your heart. Wow! That's good news!

Once you accept this truth (yes, the choice is yours),
you will begin to walk in what the Bible calls the "new-
ness of life" (Romans 6:4). And I said walk, not run.
Walk. Step by step by step ("Walk by the Spirit, and you
will not carry out the desire of the flesh" [Galatians
5:16]).

When I married Bill, I did not automatically become
what you might call the ideal wife. I wanted—no, it ran
deeper than a want—I was *determined* to be a perfect wife,
yet I look back on those first years and shudder: gross
money mismanagement, tinted whites, inedible culinary
delicacies. It was far from perfect, but a learning process—
a difficult one to be sure—had begun. I was playing a new
role—wife. I left my old identity as a single behind and
read how-to books on everything from fluffy omelettes and
flaky crusts to fulfilling sex. Everything changed with my
new identity, with my new job description.

The process is no different with the new role you
have acquired as a new creation in Christ. (Remember the
first question? "How willing are you to abandon your
past?") You leave your old identity behind. The patterns
you developed as you interacted with the people in your
world and your environment throughout the years, what
happened to you in your past, you choose to leave that
behind and begin to learn, to discover, who you became
when you were reborn—*who you are now* (see "My True
Identity," pages 72-76).

"But Anabel, I don't *feel* different; I don't *feel* like a new creation."

Welcome to the club. Read this carefully: *Nowhere in Scripture are we promised that we will feel a certain way.* If you wait until you feel like a new creature (looking to your emotions as the barometer of truth), you will never walk in the Spirit, you will never know true release from those habit patterns you have lived in all your life, you will never know real victory. "We walk by *faith*, not by *sight*" (2 Corinthians 5:7). And what is it that we believe by faith (not by sight or by how we feel)?

Christ Lives in You

"Your body is the temple (the very sanctuary) of the Holy Spirit Who lives within you" (1 Corinthians 6:19, AMP). Therefore, nothing can come into your life that He is incapable of handling. "Nothing is too difficult for Thee" (Jeremiah 32:17). God, dwelling in you, is more than a conqueror. "We overwhelmingly conquer through Him who loved us" (Romans 8:37).

You Are a New Creation

"If any man is in Christ, he is a new creature" (2 Corinthians 5:17). You are new, but you have old patterns in your memory banks that you must recognize and choose to come against.

You Are in Christ

"I am in My Father, and you in Me, and I in you" (John 14:20). You are nestled inside love—protected and secluded.

You Are Holy

"If the root be holy, the branches are too" (Romans 11:16). You are not repulsive as part of God's family; you are not under a curse as part of His body. "You are Christ's body, and individually members of it" (1 Corinthians 12:27). Christ's sacrifice on the cross established your righteousness once for all. "We have been sanctified. . . . He has perfected for all time those who are sanctified" (Hebrews 10:10-14). This is your identity.

You Are Holy, Blameless, and Irreproachable

And this is regardless of how you perform. "He has now reconciled you in His fleshly body through death, in order to present you before Him holy and blameless and beyond reproach" (Colossians 1:22). You will sin; you will, at times, be a disappointment to yourself and to God; you will not perform perfectly. But your performance does not determine your identity. Birth determines identity, and you have been reborn as a new creation.

You Are Seated in the Heavenly Places

"And raised us up with Him, and seated us with Him in the heavenly places, in Christ Jesus" (Ephesians 2:6). You are not under the circumstances; you are above them. If you maintain this perspective, you will not be destroyed by what comes into your life.

You Are Loved

"For the Father Himself loves you" (John 16:27). This gives meaning to your life; it sets you free from the frantic search for love that has controlled your thoughts and motives for years. And not only does it free you, but it also releases those around you who have been subjected to your manipulation and moods—your bartering for that precious commodity called love. They're free, too! You walk in an atmosphere of love, confident and secure. They will be amazed and will want what you have—and you will have enough to share with them.

You see, you can no longer say, "I'm not loved. No one appreciates me or the things I do." *It's not true.*

These are such simple, basic truths, and yet they are so powerful. Once we choose, by faith, to apply them, to practice them in our mind, a profound transformation will begin to take place. Oh, it won't happen overnight. If your emotions have been sitting on an eight for 37 years, it will take a while for them to come down. But you *will* notice a change. Reprogramming your computer will mean the difference between days of despair and days of peace and confidence, the difference between relationships that have simply existed for years and ones that will exude the love of Christ. It will mean walking in obedience and allowing Him to be your life. And it will mean coming to know that life at its fullest.

Is it possible that this might be the key to living?

Could this be the treasure you have been searching for?

Could this be the cure for the frustration and depression that have merged into years of unhappiness?

Yes. It is reality! It is the good news of the gospel. And remember, the measure of success you experience will depend on two things:

1. Your willingness to abandon the past.
2. Your willingness to give up *your* way for *His* way.

Lord,

You have said I am in You, that I am a new

creation, loved unconditionally, and that I am a righteous and holy person because of Your Son, Jesus.

I do not feel this to be true; I cannot see it to be real. Frankly, even Your love for me seems questionable at times.

But I choose to accept what I have read and learned here, and I say (trembling and confused) that I trust

> Your wisdom
> Your plan
> Your strength
> Your ways—I believe.

Selah

Personal Reflections

Flesh Inventory

In order to recognize the conditions that seem to describe you much of the time, place a number (from one to ten, ten being greatest) beside the following traits you identify with.

These traits were generated through walking in the world. Some are socially acceptable, some are not. They constitute your unique version of the flesh. As we will see in the next chapter, Satan, using the indwelling power of sin, will seek to control you through these patterns.

Angry at others	Anxiety
Angry at self	Argumentative
Angry at God	Astrology, horoscopes
Avoid intimacy	Bigotry
Bitterness	Blame God
Blame others	Boastful

Bossy
Bottle emotions up
Can't apologize
Can't express gratitude
Causing dissension
Complacent
Compulsion to repay
  favors done
Compulsive behavior
Compulsive thoughts
Conceit
Controlled by emotions
Controlled by peers
Control others
Covetousness
Critical attitude
Deceitful
Defensive
Demand rights
Denial
Depression
Dominance
Don't trust God
Doubt God's Word
Difficult to receive help
Drug dependency
Drink to relax
Empty religiosity
Envy
Escapism
False modesty
Fear
Fear of weakness
Feel weak/helpless
Feel inadequate
Feel inferior
Feel insecure
Feel rejected
Feel stupid

Feel superior
Feel unlovable
Feel unworthy
Feel worthless
Gluttony
Greed
Guilt (unwarranted)
Guilt (valid)
Happiness is the major
  goal
Hateful to others
Hatred
Homosexual attraction
Hostile toward God
Hostile toward others
Hostile toward self
Idolatry
If it feels good, do it
Impatient
Impulsive
Impure thoughts
Inadequate
Indifferent to others' pain
Inhibited emotionally
Insecure
Intemperance
Intimidate others
  (deliberate)
Introspective
Jealousy
Lazy
Loner
Low self-discipline
Low self-image
Lust for pleasure
Manipulate others
Materialistic
Must be in control
Must be strong

Negativism
Nervousness
Not under authority
Obsessive/compulsive
  behavior
Occult (attracted to)
Opinionated
Overly quiet
Overly sensitive to
  criticism
Overly submissive
Passivity
Passive aggressive
Perfectionist
Performance-based
  acceptance of others
Performance-based
  self-acceptance
Possessive of others/things
Prejudice
Pride
Procrastination
Profane
Project blame
Prone to gossip
Rebellion at authority
Resentment
Restlessness
Sadness
Self-absorbed
Self-condemnation
Self-depreciation
Self-gratifying
Self-hatred
Self-indulgence
Self-justification
Self-pity
Self-reliant
Self-righteous

Self-serving
Self-sufficient
Selfish ambition
Selfish with possessions
Selfish with time
Sensuality
Sexual fantasizing
Sexual lust
Silent treatment
Slow to forgive
Stubbornness
Subjective (live by feelings)
Suicidal thinking
Suspicious of God
Suspicious of others
Temper
Time consciousness
  impairment
Too quick to speak
Unbelief of God's Word
Unlovely (self-perceived)
Use threats to control others
Use blackmail to control
Use guilt to control
Use manipulation to
  control
Use money to control
Use passivity to escape
  responsibility
Vanity
Withdrawal
Workaholic
Worrier

My True Identity

I've written down what each verse says about you. Read it out loud so you can hear what God is saying. And remember, we are not talking about feelings; we're talking about your *true identity*. You might like to highlight these phrases—and the others you will find on your own—in your Bible.

John 1:12	I am a child of God. (Romans 8:16)
John 15:1,5	I am a part of the *true* vine, a channel (branch) of His life.
John 15:15	I am Christ's friend.
John 15:16	I am chosen and appointed by Christ to bear His fruit.
Acts 1:8	I am a personal witness of Christ for Christ.
Romans 3:24	I have been justified and redeemed.
Romans 5:1	I have been justified (completely forgiven and made righteous) and am at peace with God.
Romans 6:1-6	I died with Christ and died to the power of sin's rule in my life.
Romans 6:7	I have been freed from sin's power over me.
Romans 6:18	I am a slave of righteousness.
Romans 6:22	I am enslaved to God.
Romans 8:1	I am forever free from condemnation.
Romans 8:14,15	I am a son of God (God is literally my "Papa"). (Galatians 3:26; 4:6)

Romans 8:17	I am an heir of God and fellow heir with Christ.
Romans 11:16	I am holy.
Romans 15:7	Christ has accepted me.
1 Corinthians 1:2	I have been sanctified.
1 Corinthians 1:30	I have been placed in Christ by God's doing; Christ is now my wisdom from God, my righteousness, my sanctification, and my redemption.
1 Corinthians 2:12	I have received the Spirit of God into my life that I might know the things freely given to me by God.
1 Corinthians 2:16	I have been given the mind of Christ.
1 Corinthians 3:16; 6:19	I am a temple (home) of God; His Spirit (His life) dwells in me.
1 Corinthians 6:17	I am joined to the Lord and am one spirit with Him.
1 Corinthians 6:19,20	I have been bought with a price; I am not my own; I belong to God.
1 Corinthians 12:27	I am a member of Christ's body. (Ephesians 5:30)
2 Corinthians 1:21	I have been established in Christ and anointed by God.
2 Corinthians 2:14	He always leads me in His triumph in Christ.
2 Corinthians 5:14,15	Since I have died, I no longer live for myself, but for Christ.
2 Corinthians 5:17	I am a new creation.
2 Corinthians 5:18,19	I am reconciled to God and am a minister of reconciliation.

2 Corinthians 5:21	I am the righteousness of God in Christ.
Galatians 2:4	I have liberty in Christ Jesus.
Galatians 2:20	I have been crucified with Christ, and it is no longer I who live, but Christ lives in me. The life I am now living is Christ's life.
Galatians 3:26,28	I am a child of God and one in Christ.
Galatians 4:6,7	I am a child of God and an heir through God.
Ephesians 1:1	I am a saint. (1 Corinthians 1:2; Philippians 1:1; Colossians 1:2)
Ephesians 1:3	I am blessed with every spiritual blessing.
Ephesians 1:4	I was chosen in Christ before the foundation of the world to be holy and without blame before Him.
Ephesians 1:7,8	I have been redeemed, forgiven, and am a recipient of His lavish grace.
Ephesians 2:5	I have been made alive together with Christ.
Ephesians 2:6	I have been raised up and seated with Christ in heaven.
Ephesians 2:10	I am God's workmanship, created in Christ to do His work that He planned beforehand that I should do.
Ephesians 2:13	I have been brought near to God.
Ephesians 2:18	I have direct access to God through the Spirit.
Ephesians 2:19	I am a fellow citizen with the saints and a member of God's household.

Ephesians 3:6	I am a fellow heir, a fellow member of the body, and a fellow partaker of the promise in Christ Jesus.
Ephesians 3:12	I may approach God with boldness and confidence.
Ephesians 4:24	I am righteous and holy.
Philippians 3:20	I am a citizen of heaven.
Philippians 4:7	His peace guards my heart and my mind.
Philippians 4:19	God will supply all my needs.
Colossians 1:13	I have been delivered from the domain of darkness and transferred to the Kingdom of Christ.
Colossians 1:14	I have been redeemed and forgiven of all my sins. The debt against me has been cancelled. (Colossians 2:13,14)
Colossians 1:27	Christ Himself is in me.
Colossians 2:7	I have been firmly rooted in Christ and am now being built up and established in Him.
Colossians 2:10	I have been made complete in Christ.
Colossians 2:11	I have been spiritually circumcised. My old, unregenerate nature has been removed.
Colossians 2:12,13	I have been buried, raised, and made alive with Christ, and totally forgiven.
Colossians 3:1	I have been raised with Christ.
Colossians 3:3	I have died, and my life is now hidden with Christ in God.

Colossians 3:4	Christ is now my life.
Colossians 3:12	I am chosen of God, holy and dearly loved. (1 Thessalonians 1:4)
1 Thessalonians 5:5	I am a child of light and not of darkness.
2 Timothy 1:7	I have been given a spirit of power, love, and discipline.
2 Timothy 1:9	I have been saved and called (set apart) according to God's purpose and grace. (Titus 3:5)
Hebrews 2:11	Because I am sanctified and am one with Christ, He is not ashamed to call me His.
Hebrews 3:1	I am a holy partaker of a heavenly calling.
Hebrews 3:14	I am a partaker of Christ.
Hebrews 4:16	I may come boldly before the throne of God to receive mercy and find grace to help in time of need.
1 Peter 2:5	I am one of God's living stones and am being built up as a spiritual house.
1 Peter 2:9,10	I am a part of a chosen race, a royal priesthood, a holy nation, a people of God's own possession.
1 Peter 2:11	I am an alien and stranger to this world I temporarily live in.
1 Peter 5:8	I am an enemy of the devil. He is my adversary.
2 Peter 1:4	I have been given His precious and magnificent promises by which I am a partaker of the divine nature.
1 John 3:1	God has bestowed a great love on me and called me His child.

5

Steps and Exits

No temptation has overtaken you but such as is common to man; and God is faithful, who will not allow you to be tempted beyond what you are able, but with the temptation will provide the way of escape also, that you may be able to endure it (1 Corinthians 10:13).

I was beginning to see who I was in Christ and how to reprogram my computer, but I continued to struggle with the sometimes stark contrast between what I knew to be true and the way I responded to certain thoughts that ran through my mind.

I was teaching from 1 Corinthians 10:13 when Carol made her, shall we say, *unexpected* remark.

"Mrs. Gillham, that verse of Scripture is not true."

I wonder how many of us—if we were very honest—would blurt out a statement like that? I have to admit, 1 Corinthians 10:13 has not always *seemed* true in my life. I feel I have been "tempted beyond what I was able." Tempted and fallen, in fact. Fallen and done irreparable damage to my dreams—my friends—my family—my life.

What happens? Why do we fall? Irreparably . . . perhaps.

I'd like to tell you about Mari. I had talked with her twice. She was 21 years old and beautiful: slender with honey-colored hair that curled just enough; her eyes were ice blue with ridiculously long (and real) eyelashes; her complexion, flawless; beautiful teeth, delightful smile. She was altogether lovely, but Mari didn't think so. In her words, she was a "real loser."

Mari told me about her relationship with her mom: "Mother is on my back constantly. I can't do *anything* right! If I mash the potatoes, there's a lump; if I iron the shirts, she always finds a dry spot; when I make the bed, she *will* find a wrinkle. I've even seen her move the divan and show me some lint to prove that I didn't vacuum well. . . ."

Don't blame Mari's mother. She had been patterned to be very strong, domineering, and outspoken, and to demand perfection from everyone around her. She had a volatile temper, and when your performance disappointed her, you knew without a shade of doubt what you had done wrong, what a "mess" you had made of things, and what she thought about it.

Mari had a sister named Jan. Jan was Miss Right and Mari was Miss Wrong. Their mother constantly compared the two, and Mari was always found wanting. Jan's

"C" in social science got this response from Mom: "Jan, dear, a "C"? That's one of your favorite subjects! How could that be? Well, don't you worry about it, darling. I'll go visit your teacher and see about getting that grade changed. I'll take care of this." And Mari's "C" in western civilization? "Mari, what have you been doing in that class? It's obvious you have *not* been applying yourself. You are grounded for two weeks, young lady, and if . . ."

Mari's dad was an extremely passive man. He never took Mari out on a "date"; he never held her in his lap and talked to her about what was happening in her life; he never took her to the park just for the fun of it; he never held her hand or touched her. He didn't have time for Mari—he was too busy trying to survive in a house with a domineering, outspoken wife. He finally decided to leave.

Now, as a child, Mari couldn't interpret this abandonment from her father's perspective: *Poor Dad, he just reached the point where he couldn't stand any more of Mom's bossiness.* No. She concluded, *If Dad had loved me, he wouldn't have left me.*

Mom tried to kill herself when Dad left, and, once again, Mari could not interpret this from Mom's point of view: *Poor Mom, she realized what she had done to Dad all these years.* No. She concluded, *If Mom loved me, she wouldn't try to leave me.*

By the time I met Mari, what had she learned about herself in her own private world, interacting with the people around her? What did she believe about herself? How did she feel about Mari?

I cannot please anyone. I am inadequate. I can't do anything right.

I cannot measure up to Jan. I am inferior and worthless.

I am unloved.... I am lonely.... I have been rejected.

*I am an unlovely person.... I am undesirable....
There is no hope for me.... I hate myself.... I wish I were
dead....*

One Friday afternoon, Mari was in her bathroom
getting ready for an evening out—with Susan. *No guy
would want to go out with a loser like me. I wish I looked
like Jan,* Mari thought as she faced herself in the mirror.
*She's so pretty. Her cheekbones are high, and her mouth isn't
big like mine. This horrible hair! Oh well.... It would be
fun to be going out with a guy tonight. I wouldn't know
what to do ... probably come across like a real airhead, but
it would be so nice to try. I hate myself.*

*Wonder what Susan and I will do tonight? Another
movie I guess, if there's one we haven't seen. What an exciting
life I have (sigh).*

*I hope I get that job. It isn't good to be around the
house all day by myself ... Mom at work, Jan at school. And
Dad? I don't even know where he is. Oh, I miss him so
much, so very, very much. Even if I get the job, I won't be
able to keep it.... I'll do something wrong. You'd think I
could do at least one thing right, but I've never done anything right in my life. Why should I think I could start now?*

*(Sigh) If only I could go somewhere, start all over
again ... where no one would know me. What a laugh!
Wherever I go I take me ... lovely Mari. I'll never change.
I'm unhappy, unlovely, unloved. I hate you, Mari! Do you
hear me? I hate you!*

*I can't ... I just cannot go on this way. Kill myself? ...
No one would miss me, that's for sure ... maybe Mother, just
for a little while, but she would have Jan. And I guess my
dad, but Daddy would probably never know. I could go to
the garage, close the door, and start the car.... They say it's
like falling asleep.... I've always heard ... that it's ...
that ... it's ... just ... just ... that ... easy....*

And she did.

Was there a way of escape for Mari? I found myself asking for answers: "God, show me what Paul was talking about in 1 Corinthians 10:13. I'm confused."

I believe God honored that honest petition.

A Daring Exposé

Let me begin by exposing the Deceiver, that power that seeks to control us, even to the point of killing ourselves on Friday afternoon if possible:

> I find then the principle that evil is present in me, the one who wishes to do good. For I joyfully concur with the law of God in the inner man, but I see a different law in the members of my body, waging war against the law of my mind, and making me a prisoner of the law of sin which is in my members (Romans 7:21-23).

Paraphrase—The principle is this: There is something present in me that is evil. I know I am a new creature in Jesus. I want to do good. I know the deep desire of my heart is to please Him, for I joyfully agree with the law of God in the new, inner man. But I am also aware of a different law (one that does not agree with His law) in the members of my body. It controls me. It enslaves me. There is conflict between the new creature that I am, what I deeply desire to do, and this power—this entity—that dwells in me (see Figure 5.1).

Paul considers our identity as new creations in Jesus a basic fact in these verses: ". . . the one [you and me] who wishes to do good. For I [the new creation] joyfully concur with the law of God in the inner man [the new man]." And this "evil present in [us]" is not *us* (just

Figure 5.1

because food is *present* in my house doesn't mean I live in a grocery store). We are not evil; we are "the one who wishes to do good." Paul also points out that the law of our mind is good. In his first letter to the church at Corinth, he wrote that we have the mind of Christ (1 Corinthians 2:16).

So we see that our mind is good, that the law of our mind is good. If this were not so, there would be no inner conflict, no "war" as Paul called it. War demands that there be opposing factions. In the verses above, these factions are evil versus good—the "law of sin" being evil and the "law of [our] mind" being good.

We are new (2 Corinthians 5:17); we are righteous (2 Corinthians 5:21); we are holy (1 Corinthians 3:17); and we are blameless (Colossians 1:22). But we don't always *act* that way, right? Like Paul, we don't always do what we wish to do (Romans 7:19). Why? If we are new creations, how does that happen? How does that "law of sin which is present in [our] members" cause us to end up doing "the very thing [we] hate" (Romans 7:15)?

A woman recently asked me some interesting questions (I think she and Paul would have talked for a long time over their coffee cups):

> I am so frustrated! I have done everything I know to do. I have prayed, I have studied my Bible, and my life is far from "victorious"! What do I do? Stand and stomp my foot at Satan and say no? That sounds like I'm taking on the devil myself, and I have the bloody wounds to prove that does not work.
>
> How does Christ live, as you say, "in and through me"? How will I be doing anything differently than what I am trying so hard to do now? How can Satan so completely defeat and control me? I want things to be better, but I don't have much hope that they ever will be.

There is much more than hope for this woman—there are *answers*. Good, solid, tested answers—answers you and I can understand and apply to our everyday existence. Let's continue our daring exposé!

Chapters 5–8 of Romans contain the word *sin* 41 times. Now read this carefully: Forty of those times, it's a *noun*; only once is it a *verb*. For instance: "Do not go on presenting the members of your body to *sin* as instruments of unrighteousness; but present yourselves to God as those alive from the dead" (Romans 6:13, emphasis added). *Sin* is a noun in this verse, but if you interpret it as a verb (e.g., stealing), then you are going to miss a most powerful truth.

W.E. Vine, in his *Expository Dictionary of New Testa-*

ment Words, points out that in 11 of these 40 instances the word *sin* is a "governing power or principle" which is "personified." What does that mean? It means that this "law of sin" is represented as a *person!* Romans 6:13 is not exhorting us not to sin—it is exhorting us not to submit to this power, this personification, this law of sin.

Satan's Game Plan

So why do we wind up doing the very thing we hate, the very thing we are exhorted *not* to do? Because we are deceived. John called Satan, the one "who deceives the whole world" (Revelation 12:9). He is the Deceiver, and he deceives us, the new creations in Christ, the ones who want to do good. The personified power of sin is the messenger boy who carries out Satan's battle strategy in this war being waged against the law of our minds, and here is how he does it.

Satan's game plan hinges on deception, and his goal is to keep us from experiencing the life that is ours in Christ, and to prevent us *at any cost* from realizing true peace and victory. For example, I've shared with you some facts (indisputable evidence) from God's Word concerning your true identity and the power of Christ which lives within you. I have told you that these facts will literally revolutionize your life if you appropriate them (take them for your own use).

Satan doesn't want you to take them for your own use; he doesn't want you to walk in these truths. They'll bring peace and joy into your life; they'll bring you victory. So he wars against the law of your mind, and he does this through your *thought-life*. Satan's access to your thought-life is through the power of sin "in the members of [your] body" (literally, your flesh and bone), and he operates by giving you thoughts, generally with first-person, singular pronouns (*I, me, my, myself,* and *mine*).

These thoughts will correlate perfectly with your unique version of the flesh (your old ways, your old habit patterns) and will be disguised as the way you have *always thought,* the way your computer has been programmed. His success comes when you, because the thoughts are so familiar, so "like you," *accept* these thoughts. Then he has you, and you wind up doing the very thing you don't want to do (see Figure 5.2).

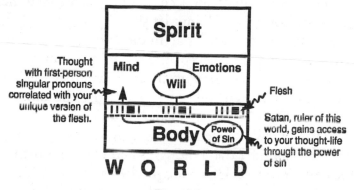

Figure 5.2

If you aren't aware of his game plan, he can easily convince you of anything—even suicide. He can convince you that the old you wasn't really crucified with Christ at all, or that she has come back to life again: *I'm not a new person! I only have to look at all the garbage in my life to know that. New creation—ha! I don't even read the Bible that much. I'm not good at my job. I'm not a good wife—I'm more of an embarrassment to my family than anything else. Everyone would be better off without me. . . .*

Examine those statements carefully. Do you see the pronouns? *I, my, me.* My dear one, these are not your thoughts. A new creation, one with the very *mind* of Christ, does not, indeed *cannot*, generate such thoughts. The "old self" is dead (memorize Romans 6:6 and Galatians 2:20). You are not fighting a civil war—the good you against the bad you. It's you, "the righteousness of God in Christ" (2 Corinthians 5:21), against "the power of sin waging war against the law of [your] mind and making [you] a prisoner of the law of sin which is in [your] members"! (Romans 7:23).

So if we are not responsible for generating these thoughts, where does our accountability come in? When *are* we responsible? "Do not let sin reign in your mortal body" (Romans 6:12). It's all in the *letting*. If we choose with our free will to accept the thoughts submitted by Satan, through the power of sin, as though they were our own thoughts, then and only then do they become our thoughts. Once we receive them and make them ours, we are entirely responsible for sinning in our thought-lives. And if we ponder these thoughts and entertain them at the conscious level long enough, they will invariably influence our will (our freedom of choice). We will choose to behave in response to those thoughts and will wind up doing the very thing we didn't want to do in the first place. We will wind up sinning.

Satan knows our old ways, our flesh. He was instrumental in their programming. But we have exposed him and how he works. We now have the information necessary to intercept his passes. *We don't have to be deceived any longer.* We can't stop him from giving us thoughts; he can give us 4,576 thoughts a day for the rest of our days. *But we don't have to accept them.* Even though they come at us with first-person singular pronouns, they are not our thoughts until we choose to make them ours.

Let's see just how Satan might put his program to work. Perhaps you were sexually molested when you were a little girl. That traumatic experience was seared into your memory banks and became a part of your *flesh*, those patterns of thought, emotions, or behavior that influence your everyday existence as a result of what happened to you in your private world. The thoughts Satan—the Deceiver—will give you will be tailor-made to keep those abusive experiences fresh in your mind, ruining your sexual relationship with your husband or fooling you into thinking of yourself as dirty, guilty, and not worth being loved by someone "nice."

You may not have suffered sexual abuse, but perhaps you were emotionally abused and, as a result, have come to see yourself as inferior and worthless. You will receive thoughts from the power of sin that "prove" or convince you of your inferiority and worthlessness. The little girl whose daddy vented his irritation at her by telling her again and again, "Any dummy ought to be able to do that!" believes herself to be a dummy. She'll even *act* like one because, after all, that's what she learned about herself and that's how she feels. The thoughts the Deceiver will give to her will keep those cruel words at the surface and always ready to validate her poor performance.

Oh, my dear, dear sister in Christ—please understand that *you do not have to accept these thoughts any longer.* You are a beautiful new creature in Christ, and He longs for you to allow Him to love you and enable you to overcome your past.

The Battle Plan

Do you remember the woman's questions I mentioned earlier? "What do I do? Stand and stomp my foot

at Satan and say no?" Well, yes . . . and no. You see, the *initial* choice must be yours, but this is simply turning on the power to the machine. What must follow is a firm belief (by faith) that Christ is your life and that *He* will fight the battle *for you, through you.* (You respond in this way because of the covenant relationship you have entered into with God through Jesus Christ.) He waits until you make that choice. He *will not* impose His will upon you. This is a decision you must choose with your will to make, and it may or may not influence your emotions (they may still be stuck on an eight!). Your decision will be only as effective as you allow it to be through setting your mind on the unalterable fact that Jesus lives inside you. Only *His* strength can enable you to make this choice.

Now, let's apply these truths to 1 Corinthians 10:13. Sin is a process, a series of descents, and each step down is a matter of choice. The Christian who has a drinking problem doesn't just find herself secluded in the basement with a drink in her hand; she arrives there through a *series of choices.* First comes the thought, *I need a drink.* This is not her thought. It is coming from Satan through the power of sin, and his one goal is to deceive and destroy her. He will hit her at her weakest point (he knows her old ways, her patterns), at that precise point in time when she needs some confidence, patience, relief, release, or an easing of the pressure: *I need a drink. I can't go on. I can't stand this pressure. I can't take it. One drink won't hurt.*

When that first thought comes—*I need a drink*—something else comes, too; something God has promised in 1 Corinthians 10:13: a doorway, a "way of escape," an out, the chance to choose no. Every time Satan offers you a choice (with first-person singular pronouns), God opens a door for you to pass through. There may be 15 steps down to the basement, but there will be 15 doors of escape, too. Fifteen chances to choose no.

But how do you do it? Pull yourself up by the boot-straps and give it your best? No, you don't have to pull this off by yourself. You have appropriated something: *Jesus Christ is your strength.* He will do it for you, through you. Your job? Trust Him to do it and then choose to allow Him to do it. Let Him do it. You pursue the right course of action: You stop, you refuse, you turn, and you head the other direction, all the while believing by faith that it is His life through you, that He is your source, and that you are drawing from the power that now lives inside you.

Let's see how many steps you might have to take (and how many exits you'd pass) to get to the basement, hiding, drinking, weak, and defeated. The first thought comes in the living room: *I need a drink.* (1) You get up and go to the kitchen, (2) open the cabinet, (3) no liquor—close the cabinet, (4) go to the bedroom, (5) open your bureau drawer and get out your purse, (6) leave your house, (7) get in your car, (8) drive to the liquor store, (9) get out of your car, (10) enter the store, (11) search out the liquor you want, (12) take it to the counter, (13) pay for it, (14) leave the store, (15) get in your car, (16) drive back to your house, (17) park your car, (18) enter your house, (19) go to the kitchen, (20) open the bottle, (21) open the cabinet door and get a glass, (22) walk down the steps to the basement, (23) pour a drink, (24) raise the glass to your lips, (25) and drink.

How many opportunities did you have to refuse? To exit? To choose no? And how many of us, in whatever descent, get to step 24 and then bitterly proclaim, "First Corinthians 10:13 doesn't work for me! God, why won't

You help me? I hate this! Where are You?" Even at step 24 you can throw the glass to the floor and smash it into fragments. You don't have to take that drink; you can still choose no. With each of those 25 steps down, there were 25 "ways of escape" just as God promised there would be, and every exit passed involved a choice, *your* choice. God will never usurp your freedom to choose.

How many exits did Mari ignore on that last Friday afternoon of her life? Did she realize the Deceiver was talking to her? That he hated her and wanted to destroy her? Did she ever hear Christ saying, "Listen to Me. Look this way—over here! There's an exit. Take it!"

Please don't misunderstand what I'm saying. Escape would not have been simple; it would not have been an easy decision to take that exit. I understand because *I have been there.* But I know one thing—you must choose. Mari *chose* to listen to the voice of the Deceiver.

Whatever your descent involves, whether it is anger, alcohol, sexual promiscuity, or thoughts of self-destruction, each step down strengthens the temptation, and the chances for resistance grow less and less. Our opponent knows when our convictions aren't strong; he knows our weakness, and his attack will intensify as he senses victory. Finally, all steps and escape routes behind you, there is overt sin as you obey the very first thought, *I need a drink. . . . I could kill myself. . . .*

Let's develop another example. (Now, if *I* can pretend back this far, surely *you* can.)

I'm a young girl, 17 years old. The guys at church seem so immature, so tame. But there's this senior at school who is Mr. Wonderful! *If only* he *would ask me for a date.* But maybe it's just as well; his reputation isn't all that great, and my stomach turns over if he even glances my way. So I content myself with 2:45 every afternoon between Band and English when I pass him in the hallways. He never notices me, but I always watch him until he disappears behind the lockers by the gym.

Then one day he actually *speaks* to me as we pass in the hall! My girlfriend and I talk for an hour that night about how completely awesome he is. And then, miracle of miracles, the next day he asks me for a date to the movies on Friday night. I coyly accept.

By the time he arrives on Friday evening, I'm so excited I'm floating! He walks me to the car and closes my door. We head downtown and drive right by the dear old Victory Theater.

"I thought we were going to the movies," I say.

"Oh, I checked around, and everyone said it wasn't worth seeing, so I thought we'd just drive around for a while. I'd like to get to know you better."

At this point in time, while I am still of sound mind, my first "way of escape" is offered to me. A warning system goes off (the temptation is so subtle). Thoughts come fast and furiously:

This isn't the way I had planned the evening. . . .

Silly girl, what's wrong with doing something other than the movie?

I told Mother and Dad I was going to the movies.

What they don't know isn't going to hurt them. . . .

These thoughts are coming to me from two sources: Satan (through the power of sin) and the Holy Spirit. I evaluate the thoughts and, with my free will, choose to act. This takes all of maybe five seconds, but within those few seconds lies my way of escape, my chance to say, "I'd really like to see the movie." It's my opportunity to exit gracefully through the side door God promised would be there. It's my cue, and I'm on stage.

"Okay," I say. We make the drag a few times—Fincher's Department Store, the 505 Cafe, see who's sitting on the rail at the Lowery Hotel—and then we head north toward the lake.

"Where are we going now?"

"I just wanted to get away from the traffic. That way I can give you my undivided attention."

Oh, these unexpected diversions! There's another door, another way of escape, another chance to choose no. The thought-game intensifies:

I don't want to be another statistic.

Hey, I'm a big girl now, I can take care of myself!

I don't like the way this is going. I wish I had never said I'd go out with him.

Come on, nothing's going to happen that I can't handle!

The exit isn't quite as wide, and the time span is shorter, but I'm still able to exercise my convictions. There's my cue again—the spotlight is trained on me.

"Okay," I say. We drive leisurely toward the lake and turn onto the infamous "Lover's Lane." "Where are we going?"

"Let's see if we can spot anyone we know."

Another opportunity to exit. My resistance is weaker and that tug-of-war in my mind is still going on:

Why don't I just casually say, "I'd like to go home, please"?

He'd never ask me out again!

Big deal! I wouldn't care.

Oh, come on, why should I be afraid? Nothing is going to happen.

My adversary knows, by now, that my convictions aren't very strong, doesn't he? The time is shorter—maybe two brief seconds. Center stage. Once again I say, "Okay."

We turn into a beautiful parking place . . . the cool breeze, soft music, shimmering moonlight. His arm is around me, his lips are so close. "Let's talk for a while. I hardly know you, and I don't like it that way." From my mouth comes a quiet, "Okay," and here I am, doing things I had no intention of doing—things I don't *want* to do. "Lord, You promised me You would not allow me to be tempted beyond the point of my endurance! You promised me a way of escape! Help!"

But how many ways of escape did I pass up? With each step down into sin, how many exits did I "okay" my way past? God kept His promise—*my decisions* brought me to the lookout at "Lover's Lane."

All sinful acts are made up of a sequence of events. Anger does not just flare up; it has been building throughout the days, the weeks, the months, the years. Pornographic magazines don't just appear in your garage. They are hiding there as a result of a series of steps, steps past doors that were there for you to open and walk through. *It's not hurting anyone,* begins the first thought. *I have a right for a little relaxation, don't I? Everybody has some little vice.* Recognize that voice? It's the voice of the power of sin, the Deceiver. We're back to the first-person-singular-pronouns game. But there is always another voice quietly directing you toward the way of escape: *I will fight this battle for you. Let Me take over.* Once again, the choice is yours.

The *first thought,* the first nudge of temptation, is our call to battle stations: *I need, I want, I am.* Author Larry Christenson says in *The Renewed Mind,* "Every spiritual battle is won or lost at the threshold of the mind." I have added, "not *in* the mind."

Facing the Enemy

We have two dogs, Esther and Bo. Esther's full name is Esther Lou Gillham, and when I use her full name, she knows she's in big trouble. When I'm making hamburger patties, Esther tiptoes into the kitchen hoping to get a little tidbit. I won't hear her come in, but I sense that she's there. I talk to her gently (she's old): "No, Esther, this is not your supper. This is people food. You go on out now, and I'll feed you later." She doesn't go.

I turn to look at her, and she's smiling, tail wagging, anticipating my response to her charming performance. It irritates me that she has not been obedient. "Esther, get out of the kitchen. It's not time for you to be fed." She smiles and wags. In exasperation I raise my voice and with forceful inflection say to her, "No! Esther Lou Gillham, you go get on your cushion!" The smile fades, the tail tucks, and she goes out the way she came in— on tiptoes. She heard me say no and could tell I was serious about that command.

Anyone with any amount of intelligence at all will recognize when no means no.

There were five us there, scattered from one corner of the big, old house on Main Street to the other.

"Supper's ready," I called.

Nothing. So I called again, only louder. Then I yelled, "Come on! It's on the table!"

I walked through the breakfast room into the foyer of the house, and there, to my complete surprise, stood a young man with attaché case in hand.

"Well, hello. Who are you?"

"I'm your vacuum cleaner salesman."

"What are you doing in my house?"

"I knocked and thought I heard someone yell, 'Come in,' so I stepped in."

Now, the way to deal with door-to-door salesmen is at the threshold—*never* in the foyer. You answer the door (with your body blocking the entrance), and you say, "Thank you for coming by. I appreciate your product, and should I ever need a new sweeper, I'll get in touch with you." And you *close* the door.

But this salesman was *in* the house. He had stepped past the threshold, and before I knew it, he had his "experimental trash" scattered all over the carpet. It took time and several stern imperatives to convince that aggressive young salesman that I was not interested in his sweepers and then to shoo him out of my house.

Dealing with the tempting thought that comes from Satan is much the same. You don't open the door and shyly suggest that the "salesman" leave. You don't allow him access to your "foyer." You say, "No!" very emphatically and close the door *before* he gets in the "house" (see Figure 5.3).

The moment you allow that thought past the threshold, not only is sin conceived, but it also takes a lot more effort to get it out once it's inside! Remember, now, that the thought you confront at the threshold of your

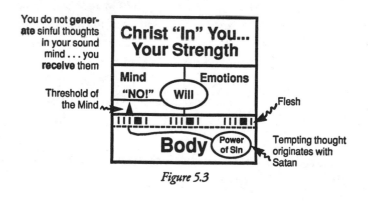

Figure 5.3

mind does not constitute sin on your part. *It is not even your thought.* It is the temptation served up to you by the power of sin under the control of Satan. You do not generate sinful thoughts in your sound mind—you *receive* them. It becomes your thought once you *choose* to receive it, to allow it past the threshold. From that point on, you are responsible for sinning.

Believing that every spiritual battle is won or lost at the threshold of the mind is a fantastic defense weapon, but how do we *know* that a certain thought is from the power of sin? How do we discern whether a particular thought should be intercepted at the threshold? We sincerely *want* to take "every thought captive to the obedience of Christ" (2 Corinthians 10:5), and though some thoughts are obviously from the Deceiver, others are very subtle.

One of the most effective methods of discernment is to know the truth; then, when a thought comes that is *contrary* to the truth, you can quickly identify it as a lie, coming from your enemy, the "father of lies" (John 8:44).

For example, if the thought condemns you, defaming your character, remember Romans 8:1: "There is therefore now no condemnation for those who are in Christ Jesus." *I'm such a lousy wife. I guess it's because I'm such a loser as a Christian. I fail at so many things. I'm inferior, unhappy, and no one loves me. My family would be better off without me . . .* ad infinitum! But wait! Those thoughts are designed to destroy you. Granted, your performance may not be that great, but you are a new creature with Christ as your very life, and you're working together on this performance routine.

You didn't generate those thoughts, and God certainly didn't give them to you. How do you know? God will not condemn you. He will not defame your character. He will *convict you of* your poor performance, but Satan will *condemn you for* your poor performance. Do you see the difference? When those thoughts come, you say, "Go peddle your lies somewhere else, Satan. I know who I am, and I'm not buying your trash."

If the thought you receive excuses or justifies your anger, remember James 1:19: "But let everyone be quick to hear, slow to speak and slow to anger." If the thought encourages your ability to handle things independently from the power of Christ, remember John 15:5: "Apart from Me you can do nothing." If the thought suggests immoral behavior, remember 1 Thessalonians 4:3: "For this is the will of God, your sanctification; that is, that you abstain from sexual immorality." If the thought implies that your future is hopeless, remember Jeremiah 29:11: " 'For I know the plans that I have for you,' declares the LORD, 'plans for welfare and not for calamity to give you a future and a hope.'" Use *truth* to detect *deception.*

Another way to ascertain the origin of a thought is to tack the phrase "in Jesus' name" to it. *I just cannot endure this one more second . . . in Jesus' name. I'm such an inferior person . . . in Jesus' name. I've had all that I can stand, and I intend to tell him so . . . in Jesus' name. I can handle this by myself! I don't need God or anyone else to help me . . . in Jesus' name. He doesn't love me. No one has ever loved me, and no one ever will . . . in Jesus' name.* The source of a thought is obvious once you ask Jesus to sanction it, isn't it?

Looking back at those years when my depression was at its peak, the thoughts I would receive (and still receive to this day) centered on *me*, on *my* rights (how they had been violated), and on defaming *my* character.

To break down this stronghold in my life, to get the sales-man out of my house (he'd been living there for years!), I had to recognize my sin. True, I wasn't maliciously hurt-ing anyone else, but I was denying the power of Christ within me and was hindering the work of His Spirit through me.

I had to *recognize* that the thoughts deceiving me into depression were coming from the power of sin, and I had to *refuse* to let them enter my mind. I could no longer invite these thoughts in and entertain them in the parlor. I had to "*reckon* myself dead to the power of sin and alive to the power of Christ" in my life (Romans 6:11); then, I had to *rest* (and that's not a *feeling* of rest; I had to *choose* to rest in what I knew despite what my emotions were doing), believing that Jesus in me was quite capable of handling the circumstances. There is no way around it—you must ultimately *choose* to win the battle.

Four Steps

It was close to midnight, January 6, 1972. My pil-low was literally damp with tears. I had retreated to bed early, but sleep was far away. I was only there to isolate myself. I *knew* what was happening: I was fighting a battle—an intense battle—for the control of my mind. I was fighting depression.

I could almost hear God saying, "Anabel, the victory is yours—all you must do is appropriate it."

"But I've been hurt, Lord," I'd say. "Bill has no right to play with my emotions, to treat me this way! He delights in tearing me down. He's wrong, Lord, *wrong!*"

The thoughts at my threshold were not new to me: resentment, anger, self-pity, bitterness, and self-destruc-tion.

If you have known depression in your life, then no doubt you're familiar with the process: It *feels* good to be sorry for yourself, to release the emotions that have caused every nerve to be taut. But that release brings total exhaustion. Numbness. Weariness.

To resist seemed impossible—but then, did I even *want* to resist?

Again the door of escape: "Bill is My responsibility, Anabel. I'm working in his life. Let *Me* handle him. Right now, claim your victory over this circumstance."

A choice was in the making. The covers were like lead. They were *so* heavy, and I was so tired. With great effort I forced myself out of bed and went downstairs to my desk. If you had been watching, you would have thought I was sick. Staggering. Stopping to hold on to the bannister. There was a war raging.

I sat down and began reading my Bible, compelling myself to concentrate on Him and to claim His power in me, through me. I took the reins of my mind; I read, praising and thanking Him, refusing to allow the twisted thoughts to come in, trusting Him, rereading—staying my mind on Him.

I signed my journal: *12:45 A.M., Victory. Thank You, Jesus.*

I made several mistakes that night, the most detrimental of which was my choice to rendezvous with the Deceiver. I chose to meet the circumstances on his terms (in bed, under the sheets, crying, feeling sorry for myself). I should have said no the moment he knocked, the moment he appeared at the threshold. I didn't. The Lord says, "Let Me handle this, Anabel. The battle isn't yours, it is Mine" (2 Chronicles 20:15b). I realized my victory when I chose to let Him do the fighting for me, when I confessed, "This is *not* the way I want to behave! This is *not* what I want. And besides that, this behavior is not consistent with who I am in Christ Jesus. *Therefore, I will not accept the thoughts being given to me by the power of sin!*" I trusted God for the strength, and I chose to act.

Four steps. That's all it takes.

1. Recognize the thought as sin. Recognize it as defamatory, as selfish, condemning, attacking your character, accusing or confusing you. Recognize it as what it is: the Deceiver's tool, a lie, a destructive thought.

2. Refuse to accept the thought as yours, and don't dwell on it. You know where it's coming from.

3. Reckon yourself dead to the power of sin (Romans 6:7; Colossians 3:5). Just as though you were a dead person, do not respond to the power of sin's suggestion.

4. Rest in knowing that you are *in* Christ and He is *in* you. And when you fail, when you fall, don't spend the rest of the day receiving thoughts about how you hate yourself, allowing the power of sin to do instant replays, going over and over what you should have done but didn't do. Remind yourself of who you are in Christ, dust yourself off, confess that you listened to the Deceiver and actually believed his lies. Tell God you're sorry, learn from your mistake, realize how you were deceived, and go on about life—walking with the poise and confidence of a woman who knows she is deeply loved, totally forgiven, and completely able to live life. *All because of Christ Jesus.*

You will guard him and keep him in perfect and constant peace whose mind (both its inclination and its character) is stayed on You, because he commits himself to You, leans on You, and hopes confidently in You (Isaiah 26:3, AMP).

6

Love Letters and Envelopes

God's Word, the Bible, is His "love letter"—His message to you. It's special. It's real. And it's essential.

There is a battle going on for the control of our minds. And our thoughts lead to action—whether we sin or take the way of escape, whether we wind up on "Lover's Lane" with the campus Romeo or ask to be taken home earlier in the evening than we had planned.

Because Satan attacks us through our thought-life, it's important we use our minds in ways that will defeat his plans for us. The apostle Paul instructs, "Fix your thoughts on what is true and good and right. Think about things that are pure and lovely, and dwell on the fine, good things in others. Think about all you can praise God for and be glad about" (Philippians 4:8, TLB).

I've discovered a creative way to "fix your thoughts." I'd like to tell you about it.

Not for "Children Only"

There are so many worlds open to us when we're little. The "dog days" of August can send us to the lush jungles, fighting mosquitoes and headhunters; the narrow confines of our postage-stamp backyard can engulf all of Alaska; and the dining room table becomes our spaceship to Venus. Can you "play-like" with me? I'm six and you're seven.

Let's pretend that we're in the mountains and there's a bad snowstorm and we're lost! And the wind is really strong and we can hardly see because of the snow! And we meet a bear and he attacks me and you fight him off to protect me!

That scenario could last all afternoon—depending on how long we were lost in the blinding snow; or how long I was able to fight the huge monster before I fell exhausted to the frozen tundra; or how long it took for you to courageously divert his attention from my lifeless body and chase him away.

When do we lose our capacity to play-like? Why is it difficult for us to close our eyes and "just imagine" when we become adults? Is the world of imagination marked "Children Only"?

I know that my own relationship with Jesus can be influenced by my willingness, or unwillingness, to use my imagination to pass the boundaries of the natural mind into God's spiritual world.

Do you remember the song, "In the Garden"? Go ever so slowly and picture it in your mind:

I come to the garden alone,
while the dew is still on the roses;
and the voice I hear, falling on my ear,
the Son of God discloses.
And He walks with me and He talks with me,
and He tells me I am His own.
And the joys we share as we tarry there,
none other has ever known.

Tell me, was it dawn or dusky in "your" garden? Were the birds just waking up and cheeping? Did you smell the roses? Where did you meet Jesus? By that crepe myrtle bush? Or by the little creek? Did you walk together, or did you sit down on the bench under the tree? What were His eyes like when He told you how very much He loves you?

Imagination. *Webster's* definition: (a) the act or power of forming mental images of what is not present; (b) the act or power of creating new ideas by combining previous experiences.

What do you meditate on as you read those lines of black print on white paper in your Bible? Pause and think about it. Are you using God's gift of imagination to make the pages come alive?

When you read, "And Mary was at the foot of the cross," what do you see? Well, it's difficult because you've never really "seen" that scene, have you? But a movie producer created one for us to put into our—you're right—imagination! And suddenly I was "wailing" with Mary. There were tears on my cheeks. I was cradling the lifeless body of my beloved son in my arms there at the foot of that cross . . . enveloped in the drenching storm and the darkness that covered the earth. Oh, the despair! The desolation! I was there. I lived it. I saw it all. How? In my imagination.

This is what it means to meditate on the Word of God, allowing your imagination to put flesh and blood into the rows of black print on white paper. Let's look at one example of how using your imagination can bring the truths of Scripture to life, enlightening your understanding.

Love Letters

Let's just imagine that you are married—very happily married. Our country becomes entangled in a full-scale war. You and your husband agree that he should enlist, and so he does. Basic training lasts several weeks, and then he returns home for a brief time before being sent into active duty. How precious those few days are—and then he's gone.

You hear from him regularly for a while, but then the letters stop coming. One finally does come, but it's not from him. It's from the United States Government: "We regret to inform you that your husband has been taken as a prisoner of war."

Your husband's captors are lenient in one way: They are going to allow him to communicate with you. Once. They will permit him to write a single letter, restricting the number of pages he can use.

Now do you suppose he would write that one letter out in a flurry of scribbles? I don't. I imagine him making notes, jotting down everything he wants to say to you, remembering how you had depended on him, how you had valued his opinions and advice. He makes certain, as best he can, to anticipate your questions and the unexpected pressures that will undoubtedly arise in his absence. Then he requests permission to write his letter.

Imagine receiving that envelope and seeing his writing. He's talking to you! He's alive! He loves you. Oh, it hurts terribly because he isn't there, but at least you have his words, his encouragement, his loyalty, his love. What are you going to do with that letter? Put it in a safety-deposit box at the bank—after you've made ten copies of it, that is.

His message begins with, "I love you and I miss you." Then he writes, "Now, about the children, this is how you should work with them, and here are some suggestions for discipline. Be careful with your finances and don't cosign notes. By the way, I love you. . . . In dealing with people, there are certain things you should be aware of. . . . Check through the important papers to evaluate our insurance coverage. And by the way, remember how very much I love you. . . ."

You read those pages over and over and over again. You know right where to find that advice about finances or the children, and you read the end of the letter every night before you go to sleep: "I'll be coming back one of these days. Wait for me. Watch for me. Be faithful to me. I love you so much. . . ."

God's Word, the Bible, is His "love letter"—His one message to you. There are paragraphs where He gives you His thoughts on discipline; He talks about financial matters; there are pages concerning interpersonal relationships; and He gives advice on how to meet the myriad unexpected pressures that will undoubtedly arise in His absence.

He's alive! He has written to you! He loves you! He tells you that He's coming back one of these days: "Watch for Me. Wait for Me. Be faithful to Me." Can you *imagine* that? Incredible!

Years ago I saw a movie with Jennifer Jones and Joseph Cotton; I believe it was called *Love Letters*. The plot wasn't that unusual: A soldier came to town and swept the heroine off her feet with tender words, gifts of love, and rash promises—then he left. She wrote to him, but he wasn't interested in writing to her. It had been nothing more than a weekend fling for him. So he asked his roommate, played by Joseph Cotton, if he would take on her letters as a project and answer them for him. Joseph agreed. Well, Jennifer fell in love with the man who wrote her the love letters. The theme song is still around:

> Love letters straight from your heart
>> keep us so near while apart.
> I'm not alone in the night
>> when I can have all the love you write.
> I memorize every line,
>> I kiss the name that you sign.
> And then darling I read again,
>> right from the start,
> Love letters straight from your heart.[1]

As you've read God's love letter to you, there are probably certain paragraphs so special that you've under-lined them, highlighted them, or put an asterisk beside them—they linger like an old song. John 14 is hopelessly dotted with highlights and ink marks in my Bible—like John 14:1,2: "Let not your heart be troubled; believe in God, believe also in Me. In My Father's house are many dwelling places; if it were not so, I would have told you; for I go to prepare a place for you"; John 14:6: "I am the way, and the truth, and the life"; and John 14:27: "Peace

I leave with you; My peace I give to you; not as the world gives, do I give to you. Let not your heart be troubled, nor let it be fearful."

I wonder if you have highlighted or underlined John 14:20—perhaps my most cherished promise in this chapter: "In that day you shall know that I am in My Father, and you in Me, and I in you." The Living Bible translates the same verse this way: "When I come back to life again, you will know that I am in my Father, and you in me, and I in you."

How can that be? Oh, you could perhaps write a paper on it and explain it theologically. But theology alone can be cold . . . formal . . . pharisaical. Theology can leave onion-skin pages with underlinings and highlights, but no relationship. Theology alone is loving the letter instead of the Person who wrote the letter.

Am I saying that without imagination John 14:20 is not true? No. It is *truth*. I am saying that as we engage the power of imagination, John 14:20 will become more than "just words." It can be "life."

And how can it become life?

Let's look at it together. *In that day . . . When I come back to life again . . .* that is after the fact, the fact of His resurrection. Our faith stands on that fact. Romans 10:9: "If you confess with your mouth Jesus as Lord, and believe in your heart that God raised Him from the dead, you shall be saved." The fact. First Corinthians 15:14: "If Christ has not been raised, then our preaching is vain, your faith also is vain." The fact. Jesus then said, "You shall *know* that I am in My Father, and you in Me, and I in you." Webster gives this definition for *know:* "to recognize as valid or as a fact; to perceive with understanding and conviction." To know means to be convinced, certain; without a doubt; to understand fully.

One of the primary ways we come to *know* something is through experience, and how well I remember this one vivid learning experience. I was probably ten or eleven years old at the time, and I was cleaning up the kitchen after breakfast. We'd used the toaster and I, probably because I didn't especially want to be cleaning up the kitchen, used a little too much "jerk" when I unplugged the toaster. One of the little gold prongs broke off in the outlet. I was in for trouble unless I could right the wrong before Mother returned to the scene of the crime. I didn't know what to do (much less what *not* to do), so I took a fork . . . Need I say more? I *knew* something after that experience, and I decided then and there I would never stick a fork into an outlet again.

Maybe you've learned that your brakes don't work on wet pavement the same way they do on dry pavement. You'd heard that, but you didn't *know* it until that one rainy day when you were driving faster than usual because you were late for work.

I don't think I could change a tire. Maybe you can. You were out on a country road and had a flat. No Sir Galahad came by (even though you prayed for one), so you, through much frustration, learned how to change a tire.

And how did you come to *know* how to make a batch of chocolate chip cookies? You learned how, you made them, and now you know.

Jesus said, "When I come back to life again, you will *know*." All right, Lord, what do I know now that You have come back to life? "You will know that I am in the Father, that you are in Me, and that I am in you." Just words, unless you'll do something with me, unless you'll *come to know* with me.

Go get three envelopes of graduated sizes and a small slip of paper (see Figure 6.1). Now, on the largest of the envelopes, print *GOD*. On the next size down, print *JESUS*. On the smallest of the three, print your name. Then on your slip of paper, print *Jesus*. Now, take your large GOD envelope and place your JESUS envelope inside it. Take the envelope with your name on it and place it inside the JESUS envelope. Now take the slip of paper with Jesus printed on it and drop it into the envelope with your name on it. "When I come back to life again, you will know that I am in my Father, and you in me, and I in you."

"Look Where *You* Are"

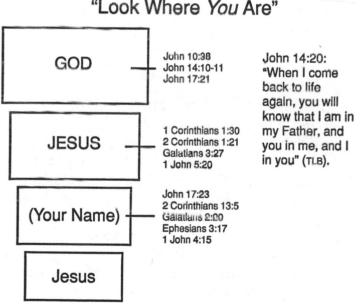

GOD — John 10:38 / John 14:10-11 / John 17:21

JESUS — 1 Corinthians 1:30 / 2 Corinthians 1:21 / Galatians 3:27 / 1 John 5:20

(Your Name) — John 17:23 / 2 Corinthians 13:5 / Galatians 2:20 / Ephesians 3:17 / 1 John 4:15

Jesus

John 14:20: "When I come back to life again, you will know that I am in my Father, and you in me, and I in you" (TLB).

"Anything that comes into my life must come through God, through Jesus, to get to me; and when it gets there, it finds me filled with Jesus, so what is there to fear?"

Figure 6.1

What an incredible picture of God and His relationship with us! Look where you are! Secure. Safe. Sheltered. Hidden. Surrounded by love.

My Hiding Place

Using the above example, it is easy to see that *anything* that comes into your life must first come through God and through Jesus before it gets to you. And when it gets there, it finds you filled with Jesus—so what is there for you to fear? How great is your God? Is anything too difficult for Him? Oh, yes, we are *in the world,* and He has forewarned us that we will have "tribulation and trials and distress and frustration" (John 16:33, AMP), but if you will only remember where you are, you will be *more than a conqueror:* "But in all these things we overwhelmingly conquer through Him who loved us" (Romans 8:37).

How "real" is John 14:20 to you now?

Very real.

Will you be forgetting it pretty quickly?

No. I'll remember it.

Why?

Because I have a picture of it in my imagination.

I have no idea where you are right now. Maybe you're reading on the bus, heading for work; maybe you're sitting in a chaise by the pool; maybe you're under the hair dryer or snuggled under the covers or at your kitchen table. Wherever you are, do you realize, now, that you aren't alone? Close your eyes and remember the illustration of the envelopes. Meditate on the fact that you are nestled inside the pockets of love with Jesus indwelling you as your very life. Such boundless wonders are not limited to six- and seven-year-olds. Your earthly circumstances cannot control the flight—the freedom—of your soul.

Hold tight to that nest of envelopes—it will remind you of where you are. It is a *promise*, a promise given to you by the One who loves you more deeply than anyone else has loved or ever will love you. And a promise of God can never be retracted. You may choose with your free will to ignore or discount John 14:20 and what it says to you. It may be powerless in your life because of your disobedience or lack of belief, but that doesn't render the promise false. It only stifles and limits the *work* of God in that you have rejected the *way* of God.

In these envelopes—John 14:20—can anything come into your life that He cannot handle? No. What about the performance of others and its impact on you? Can Jesus handle that? Of course. What about *your* performance? Can loneliness, unhappiness, or abuse destroy you? No. Because you know where you are, can you rest in His love? In His wisdom? In His strength? Yes. Can you read His love letter to you and fall more and more in love with the One who wrote it? Yes. Is He coming back someday? Yes. Will He find you still in love with Him? Faithful to Him? Waiting for Him? Expecting Him? Yes.

And still reading His letter.

7

That's Not What I Meant!

I wonder if the Lord ever experiences exasperation at our inability to understand? If He is ever amazed at our interpretation of what He has so carefully written? If He ever just shakes His head and mutters to Himself, "That's not what I meant."

I thought I was ready to be a wife when I took a husband on that lovely, leafy October day. I *knew* I could handle everything that would be expected of me—no debating the issue. It didn't take long for me to discover that I wasn't nearly as ready as I thought I was; but then, I had my husband, the self-appointed critic, to keep that ever before me. "You are not doing it the way I want you to do it," he would say.

I had the same mind-set in my Christian walk—*I can do it*. And I tried, and I tried, and I tried. Granted, I didn't have someone evaluating my every move, keeping me off balance with criticism, but I am confident that God would often, while observing my "perfect" performance, shake His head and mutter, "Oh, Anabel. That's not what I meant."

Ahead of His Time

Just when Moses discovered that his roots were Hebrew and that he wasn't an Egyptian prince is not recorded in the Scriptures. The writer of Acts tells us that "Moses was educated in all the learning of the Egyptians, and he was a man of power in words and deeds" (7:22). According to the verses that follow, when he was nearing the age of 40, he decided it was time for him, as the person through whom God would grant His people deliverance, to begin his work, to be all God wanted him to be. He decided that he was ready.

He began by killing an Egyptian he saw abusing a fellow Israelite. But this one-on-one extermination approach wasn't too successful. The following day, he ran for his life to Midian where he fell from prince to pauper, tending sheep in the desert instead of being a leader among men (Acts 7:20-29; see also Exodus 3:1).

Moses thought he was ready; after all, he *was* a "man of power in words and deeds." It would seem that during those 40 years in Pharaoh's palace he had learned one thing very well: "I can do it! I have been well-trained. I have conquered in battle. I have great power and strength. I will be the deliverer, the savior who will set my brothers free." And all the while God was shaking His head, muttering, "Moses, that's not what I meant."

When he decided to help God, Moses wasn't wrong in his vision, in his dreams, or in his goal. *His method was wrong. His perception of how God worked and of God's ways was wrong.* Moses didn't really *know* what God wanted him to be, and it took another 40 long years for God to build *new* patterns into Moses and bring him to that understanding. God wanted a man who was aware of his inadequacies; a man who, of necessity, would draw from God's strength, wisdom, and power; a man who would recognize God's ability through his own weakness.

Dear Moses learned. After those 40 years in Midian, the Scriptures tell us, "Now the man Moses was very humble, more than any man who was on the face of the earth" (Numbers 12:3). How many experiences of failure do you suppose the man Moses had to endure throughout those 40 years of exile until he came to see that he wasn't ready to be all God wanted him to be? Can you comprehend the Moses of Pharaoh's palace saying, "Lord, I'm such a nobody. No one would pay me any mind. I have never been eloquent. I've never been able to communicate successfully. I can't think of things to say or even say them once I've thought of them. Don't ask me to deliver Your people! Send someone else to do it" (Exodus 3:11; 4:10-13)?

Ready: At Hand, Responsive, Prepared

Ron Dunn, director of Lifestyle Ministries, sums up Moses' readiness this way: "When Moses thought he was ready, he wasn't; and when he thought he wasn't ready, he was." What does it mean to be "ready" for the plans God has? For *me* to be ready? For *you* to be ready?

1. Being *ready* means being willing to be all God wants me to be, not what *I* want me to be (or what I think He wants me to be).

2. Being *ready* means being willing to do it God's way, not my way.

3. Being *ready* means being sensitive to God's direction in my life; it means meeting a need not through a sense of duty or guilt, but because of His direction, His presence, in my life.

4. Being *ready* entails confessing my weakness and relying solely on His indwelling strength.

5. Being *ready* means relinquishing all glory and praise to Him (and that's even if the results don't turn out like I think they should have turned out).

6. Being *ready* entails risking the loss of acceptance, praise, and any—or all—of the darling things I have clung to for security.

Enlightened

Like Moses, Saul of Tarsus had a goal: *to be all God wants me to be.* And what did that mean to Saul? It meant being well-informed, knowledgeable, a teacher of the law, a Pharisee; it meant being dedicated, committed, enthusiastic, zealous, a persecutor of Christians; it meant being blameless, a keeper of the law *par excellence*, the "chiefest" of the law-keepers! He wanted to be an enthusiastic disciple to whom others could look and be challenged by his flawless performance, his commitment to God. A worthy goal? Yes, a very worthy goal.

Like Moses, Saul's *motive* was not wrong—his *method* was wrong. Saul had come to believe the same things Moses came to believe, only in a different environment: one as a prince in Pharaoh's palace, one as the Pharisee of Pharisees. "I can do it!" was Paul's cry. "I have been well-trained. I know the laws of God, and I am able to keep them. I am jealous for God and protective of Him. I will be His deliverer!"

God had to break through the wall of Saul's misunderstanding: "And it came about that as he journeyed, he was approaching Damascus, and suddenly a light from heaven flashed around him; and he fell to the ground, and heard a voice saying to him, 'Saul, Saul, why are you persecuting Me?'" (Acts 9:3,4). Paraphrased—"Hey, down there! Saul! You're doing it all wrong. That's not what I meant!"

God got through to Saul. Numbed by the revelation that he had been wrong for so long, he resigned from every committee, dropped out of the choir, stopped attending teachers' meetings, visitation, Sunday school, and everything else, and isolated himself in the wilderness for three years. He had to learn what God really wanted him to be (Galatians 1:17,18). He had thought that he was ready, that he was well on the road to being all God wanted him to be, but God had to bring him to the point of true readiness.

(Do you remember what being ready means? Do you want to go back and read it again?)

And then there was Anabel Gillham. I'm not putting myself in the same company with Moses and Saul, but all three of us were well-trained, competent do-it-yourselfers. I wanted desperately to be all God wanted me to be (which is, remember, a good and godly desire). I wanted to be a leader for God, like Moses; I wanted to be that servant who others honored and esteemed because of her flawless performance, because of her commitment to God, like Saul.

But my world was in such a mess. I was struggling to keep my marriage together, or at least to keep the they're-such-a-happy-couple facade in place. And with their pliable hearts, their love, and their complete trust, I was pouring the lives of my young sons into the same mold. I had learned (indeed, been *taught*) to operate in my own strength. I was misinformed. I didn't know God's plan for my life. I was ignorant of God's definition of readiness, and all the while He was saying to me, "Anabel, that's not what I meant." He had to get through to me— He had to bring me to that point where I said, with Moses, "Lord, I can't," and with Saul, "Lord, what will You have me do?"

Where are you? How ready are you? What would your answer be?

"Be all God wants me to be? What a laugh! Me? With three preschoolers and a husband who doesn't even know God, let alone care what He wants him to be! I'm breathing through a straw, living in this dinky, dilapidated dump, and every day I'm inundated with dirty diapers (millions of them!), dirty kids, dirty dishes, dirty clothes, dirty rooms, dirty jokes—*ad nauseam!* Be all God wants me to be? Sure! In 20 years, maybe, give or take a few, depending on how many more kids I have. . . ."

"Be all God wants me to be? No hope. I had an abortion five years ago—and I was a Christian. Strange how one tragic mistake can ruin your whole life. I live with constant guilt, and I have nightmares: This child runs toward me, but he never seems to be able to reach me—and he's crying and calling, 'Mommy! I'm scared! Help me, Mommy!' Oh, how I hate myself. . . ."

"Being 'ready' is easy enough for Anabel to talk about. I'm tired of people telling me what I ought to do or how I should be when they have no idea what I'm going through. She probably jets all over the country and stays in plush hotels and eats out. Her kids are grown and gone. She has nice clothes—probably even a cleaning woman. People like her make me sick. . . ."

Please hear me. *What God wants you to be does not depend on your circumstances, the people around you, your talents, your gifts, or on making a right turn when you should have turned left.* (Did you get that?) What God wants you to be does not depend on your circumstances, the people around you, your talents, your gifts, or on making a right turn when you should have turned left. The world uses these very same things to control us, to defeat us, to squeeze us into its mold. But God will use them to fit us into *His* mold, to conform us into *His* image, to transform us into all He wants us to be. God is not nearly as interested in changing our circumstances as He is in changing *us* in our circumstances.

It is *crucial* (and I chose that word deliberately; it means "supremely critical; decisive") for your Christian walk indeed, for your life—that you learn what Moses and Saul learned, that you learn what I learned. You cannot be all God wants you to be until you realize—until you grasp, until you accept—the truth: *YOU cannot be all God wants you to be.*

Have you been trying for years, like Moses, giving it your best, like Saul, convinced that *you* can do it, like Anabel? In the rest of this book we're going to be talking about relationships with others, primarily marriage. Are you going to attempt, under your own strength, to incorporate into your life what you learn? Do you suppose God is trying to get through to you: "Hey, down there! That's not what I meant! I want to do it all for you, through you! Will you let Me?"

Letting someone else do something for you involves submission—allowing him to do it his way. But submission to God is more than the act of submission—it is an attitude: *that God's desires might become your desires.* Complete submission—the utter giving up of yourself, rights, possessions, privileges, placing yourself under His authority, agreeing with Him because you have come to know Him.

> Let them boast in this alone: That they truly know me, and understand that I am the Lord of *justice* and of *righteousness* whose *love is steadfast;* and that *I love to be this way* (Jeremiah 9:24, TLB, emphasis added).

This is God's self-portrait. These characteristics motivate Him and *always* define His ways (i.e., "I allowed this, or I did this, because I am always just and righteous and because I love you; and incidentally, I love being this way"). We *know* Him. This is the God to whom we submit.

All of our time together has been spent "discovering" where the horse belongs—in front of the cart. You must submit to God and allow Him to be where He belongs in your life before we talk about relationships, before we talk about marriage. You are first and foremost under submission to God; this is what will make your life—whether you are married or single—palatable, meaningful, and fulfilling. It is the one, necessary ingredient that will enable you to meet every circumstance victoriously.

Arrogant Warrior

Do you remember the story of Naaman (2 Kings 5)? He was highly respected, he was a mighty warrior, he was the commander of King Aram's army, he was a great man in the sight of his master, and he was a leper. Nothing had ever come into Naaman's life that he could not handle. Until now. (We're back to Moses, Saul, and Anabel again—"I can do it!" Are you part of our parade?)

Naaman's wife had a little Israeli slave girl who loved enough (I don't know *who* she loved, but she could not remain silent) to suggest that her master, Naaman, go see a prophet, Elisha. "He would cure him of his leprosy," she said. A suggestion from a child? A slave? Yes. When we get desperate, we grab at the slightest hint of hope.

So Naaman went to Israel and sought out Elisha. The prophet didn't even do the mighty hero the honor of coming to the door. "Gehazi, see who's at the door, please."

Naaman was infuriated! "Who does he think he is? Does he know who I am? Who I represent?" And when the servant Gehazi gave him Elisha's instructions, telling him to go and dip seven times in the muddy Jordan River, Naaman was even more frustrated. Unthinkable! "They have beautiful rivers back in Syria. Why should I humiliate myself by doing what this man tells me to do? I will not!"

But there was one man in Naaman's group who dared to approach the arrogant warrior. "Oh, please, sir! You are here. Why not at least try to do what the prophet has told you to do? What do you have to lose?" I wonder how much courage that took? Was his heart thumping? Were his palms sweaty? "All right, all right! I'll try it, but it is utterly and absolutely ridiculous. Ridiculous!"

Searching the prophet out and telling him the

problem was not enough. Hearing the prophet's instructions was painful—it hurt his pride to think of doing something so demeaning. Naaman did not believe, but he was desperate. He did not understand the prophet's remedy, but he was hurting. He merely humbled himself and obeyed, that's all. He obeyed and that submission brought healing.

And you? Obedience. You must allow God to be *your* God—you must submit to Him before you can submit to His plan for your life, before you can be ready to be what He wants you to be. You can't do it in your own strength, either. Some of you have probably read Maribell Morgan's *The Total Woman* and, trying to *be* that total woman, have ended up with frustration, confusion, bitterness, resentment, and despair—the "totaled woman." No. There is only one way.

God Doesn't Bargain

Gene McNaughton didn't have time for God; he was too busy enjoying life. Successful in his work, respected in his community, in good health—why *should* he need God? And today he was doing what he loved to do more than anything else—bird hunting. It was cold, and that Arkansas air was biting; a new dog added to his excitement. All was well with Gene McNaughton.

His dog flushed a covey: *Not bad shooting, old boy,* Gene thought to himself, *and Sandy is retrieving just great.*

"Now drop it!" *That's bad. She isn't dropping the game.*

Gene laid his gun on the ground and proceeded to scold the excited pup. She stepped on the trigger.

Odd—one minute all's well, and the next minute Gene is lying on that cold, Arkansas ground with a gaping wound in his leg, bleeding, isolated, and no one knows where he is.

"God? I need some help down here. This is some serious stuff. I'll do anything if You'll just get me out of this mess. I'll give money to the church. I'll even start *going* to church!"

No answer. It's midday, but you can't tell it. It's getting colder, or at least it seems that way to Gene. The bleeding isn't as bad, but the pain is deep, intense.

"God, I need Your help. I agree with You—I haven't given You much thought these past years, but I plan to change all that. I really do. I'll start living my life for You—You know, my money, my job, my family, my managerial skills. I want to start using all those things for You, but I need You to take care of this one situation right now before I can start on that new plan."

No answer. It was 17 degrees last night. *If there were just some trees around instead of this open field!*

"Well, God, looks like I'm not gonna make it. That bargaining didn't impress You much, did it? Oh, well, bargaining time is over now. I've been wrong all along, and I know it. I need You, God. I need Your Son, Jesus."

Strange. A peace.

"I love You, Lord. Doesn't really matter, does it? If I don't make it tonight, I'll be with You. Thanks for loving me, for letting me come in at the last minute like this. I'm just sorry I didn't respond until I was out of it."

A farmer was heading home, driving down a little country road. *Is that a man out there? I'd better check it out. . . .*

Anabel tried bargaining. Thirty years is a long time to hold out on a deal, but I held out. I wasn't lying on the cold ground with a bloody leg that would eventually have to be amputated, as Gene's was, but I was desperate for help. I was hurting, and I finally came to the same conclusions Gene reached: "Lord, I can't get myself out of this one. You're going to have to do it all for me, and I'm trusting You, Lord. I'm not going to tell You what to do or how to do it. I just want You to know I love You."

That's being *ready*, dying to my way and placing myself under God's authority, accepting His ways and agreeing with Him because I *know* Him, because I am familiar with His character.

The decision is yours. How I cherish for you the beautiful freedom that will blossom in every area of your life should you choose to submit to *His* way.

I'm ready, Lord.

A Commitment

Dear Father,

I am Yours.

You have touched my life. I have heard Your voice. You have given Yourself to me. How I thank you for loving me and allowing me to come to You, boldly, seeking mercy, seeking grace, as Your child—born into Your family and made acceptable to You by the obedience of Your beloved Son, Jesus Christ.

I believe You speak to me through the Word, Father, and I have found in Your Word that apart from Your life I am inadequate, incapable, completely dependent on Your strength, Your wisdom, Your power. I thank You that these necessities are met through Jesus. Oh, I want so very much to be obedient to You, learning and applying the truths that You are revealing to me. But I must confess that I don't understand it all. Thank You for requiring obedience, not understanding.

I long to be used now, Jesus, by Your power, not mine. Work Your perfect will in me. I submit my will to Yours. Take me, fill me with Your beauty, that I may give and give and give again, reveling in Your love for me. I pray that You will draw me close to You. Thank You for enveloping me in Your perfect, pure love.

I'm ready, Lord.

Signed _____

Date _____

PART II

Who I Am in Relation to Others

8

What to Do with Your Balloon

Just as my child brings his broken toys
with tears
for me to mend,
I took my broken dreams to God
because He was my friend.
But then . . . instead of leaving Him
in peace
to work alone,
I hung around and tried to help
with ways that were my own.
At last I snatched them back
and cried,
"How could You be so slow?"
"What could I do, My child?" He said.
"You never did let go."

—Faith Mitchner

In the early years, having four boys around the house meant toy cars—all sizes, shapes, makes, and models. My youngest son, Wade, brought me one of his cars one day. He was probably four years old at the time. "I broke my car, Mom."

"Let me see it, Honey." Sure enough. The axle was bent, and the little car wouldn't roll. "Hey, I think I can help. I'm real good at fixing broken things. Want me to try?"

"Yes, ma'am."

So I stepped into the garage and picked up two pairs of pliers—you have to have one pair to hold the tip of the axle steady while you bend it out with the other pair (needless to say, I'd done this before)—then I went back into the kitchen where Wade was waiting and crying because *something he loved so dearly was broken beyond his ability to repair it.* He had it clutched tightly in his fist. "You want me to work on it?"

"Yes, ma'am."

"Well, then, you're going to have to let me have it in my hands." I got down on my knees so he could watch. I didn't mind his head being so close to mine or his leaning against my leg. . . .

From Laurie

My husband and I have been married almost 13 years. We never had children . . . perhaps that was a mistake. I don't know. Maybe having a baby would have drawn us closer together. It hasn't been a good marriage, but we've not argued or been hateful to each other. We've both worked. He's had his life; I've had mine. Oh, we'd go out for a meal every so often;

it's just that we didn't seem to have time for each other, and we didn't especially have anything in common.

Saturday was generally our only day together. (That's a strange word—together.) I'd fix breakfast and then work around the house while he did different things. We still weren't together I guess.

Last Saturday I was in the kitchen fixing breakfast. I had just looked at the clock—it was 9:30. When he came in I immediately noticed that he wasn't in his casual Saturday clothes, but was dressed to go out. He said, "Laurie, I have filed for divorce and there's nothing to discuss. I know this will upset you, so I'm leaving for the day."

At 9:29 A.M., I had a husband—I was fixing his breakfast, remember? At 9:30 A.M., he was gone.

And a circumstance has come into Laurie's life over which she has no control, a person she cannot control. What does she do?

From Beth

Steve is 16. He's a good-looking kid. He's not a model son, but we've always been able to talk. Why didn't he talk to me?

I had just finished the laundry, had all the clothes folded and was taking them to the various bureaus. When I opened Steve's drawer, I thought, *What a mess. . . . I'm going to clean it out for him.* I wasn't prying, Anabel. I was just being a mother. Well, I took everything out and on the bottom of the drawer were the things that told me he was into drugs. My Steve. Oh, no, no. I guess I should have known. Something's been bothering him, but I thought he'd talk to me. . . .

And a circumstance has come into Beth's life over which she has no control, a person she cannot control. What does she do?

From Marge

It's after midnight and I'm sitting at the kitchen table. Dog tired . . . whatever that means . . . and worried sick about Jenny. I still have some washing that needs to be done. Having to work late really throws me behind . . . as if I ever get caught up. There's always something yelling at me that needs to be done. Ironing. Dusting. Laundry. Shopping. And look at my nails. . . .

Davie is asleep . . . thank goodness. He's doing a little better this year in his school work. I don't think he misses his dad quite as much as he used to. He seems to be adjusting. But not Jenny.

A 17-year-old girl needs a dad to help her feel special, loved, protected . . . a dad to help her stand up to the peer pressure. The kids she's running with are no good. She's ruining her life and I can't stop her! If only I had someone to help me.

Where *is* that kid? I'll wait up for her. I can't go to bed until she gets in. Jenny, please come home. Please don't do anything bad.

Jenny, I love you . . . and I'm so sorry your father left . . . it wasn't your fault, honey.

And a circumstance has come into Marge's life over which she has no control, a person she cannot control. What does she do?

From Anabel

I had been to Poteau to visit Mother. She had been alone, now, for 11 years. We had such a good time. She had supper all ready for me when I got there: broiled chicken, a baked potato, and salad. She was such a good cook. We watched one of her favorite game shows while we ate. It was a nice visit.

We drove over to Ft. Smith for a doctor's appointment on Wednesday, then she and my sister, Betty, headed south for Poteau, and I headed north for Springfield. I can still see her turned around in the front seat, waving good-bye.

On Thursday evening, just about supper time, the phone rang. It was Betty's husband: "Belle, you'd better come back home as soon as you can. Your mother had a stroke this morning, and it doesn't look good."

And a circumstance has come into my life over which I have no control, a person I cannot control. What do I do?

I hope you have realized these amazing facts in this book so far:

1. You are totally accepted by God simply because

you are His, because you are *in* Christ Jesus. Your *performance* may gain His *approval* ("Well done, good and faithful servant" [Matthew 25:14-21]), but it will never gain His *acceptance*.

2. There is only one person who ever lived the Christian life—Jesus Christ. His Spirit now indwells you (1 Corinthians 6:19), and as you allow Him to meet life for you, you will be able to live the Christian life (not always successfully I hasten to add!). You believe by faith that He will do this (Galatians 2:20).

3. You are a new creature in Christ Jesus (2 Corinthians 5:17). You are holy, righteous, blameless, and forgiven (1 Corinthians 1:8; 2 Corinthians 5:21; Colossians 1:22; Ephesians 1:4; Colossians 2:13), with the laws of God written on your heart and mind (Hebrews 10:16).

4. God loves you unconditionally (1 John 4:10).

5. You now have the very mind of Christ (1 Corinthians 2:16b). The rebellious, destructive thoughts that come to you are coming from the power of sin. They are not your thoughts.

6. You are enveloped in God, in Jesus, with Jesus living inside you that you might meet each day in *His* power (John 14:20).

With these incredible truths beneath us, holding us up, we can go on. We're "unsinkable"! We're prepared to begin dealing with the others in our life now.

Because we've established a right relationship with God, we'll be able to establish right relationships with others. In the following chapters, we'll be looking at these relationships—in particular, marriage. We'll discover how

God can renew, restore, and revitalize what we may have given up on. And we're about to find out that the place to start is with giving our burdens for others to the Lord. Are you ready to listen . . . to learn?

Cast or Carry?

When a person comes into your life bringing his bag of problems with him, when a person carries grief and stress and pain into your world, when a person causes chaos over which you have no control, what do you do?

How do you deal with the pressure of painful encounters and fragmented relationships? With angry, rebellious people? With divorce, sickness, bitterness, and death? With loneliness? With the circumstance that you never dreamed would be a part of your life? With the weight of the burden that has worn out your emotions and left you physically exhausted? How do you handle it? How?

The Bible, our love letter, tells us in Psalm 55:22, "Cast your burden upon the Lord, and He will sustain you." Let's paraphrase that: "Get rid of that burden; throw it on the Lord; fling it at His feet. Don't sneak up to give it to Him (to cast means to throw forcefully). Once you have done that, He promises that He will take care of you, sustain you; He promises to be your sustenance."

What sort of sustenance is the psalmist talking about here? It's not physical, not food or drink. I need emotional sustenance. Emotional relief. I need stability, strength, and wisdom. I need peace, the therapy of rest. I need the calmness that comes when I *know* that everything is under the control of an authority figure, a professional, someone I can trust, someone who knows what to do. That's exactly the sort of sustenance Psalm 55:22 is talking about.

Peter, in his first letter, echoes the psalmist, "[Cast] all your anxiety upon Him, because He cares for you" (5:7). Paraphrase: "Throw everything onto Him that is a burden to you, anything that causes you stress or anxiety. He doesn't want you to carry it. He loves you and wants to take that responsibility for you. A gentleman will do such things. Love does such things."

Most of us have tried to give our burdens to the Lord, but we can't seem to accomplish that difficult feat. We give it to Him, and five minutes later we take it back. We don't know how to take our burden to the Lord and leave it there. Do you recall my concept of God and how He viewed my burdens? "God has more than enough problems to deal with," I used to say. "Why should I dump mine on Him? What did He give me a brain for? I'm a capable person. He expects me to handle this. After all, 'God helps those who help themselves.'"

Wrong concept. God tells us—in fact, *commands* us—to cast our burdens onto Him.

Watching Over the Sacks

I had several sacks of clothing to give to the Salvation Army, so I called them and asked them to come by. Then I put the sacks on the front porch so they could pick them up regardless of whether or not I was home. They were to come on Thursday, but I got my days mixed up and thought they were to come on Wednesday. They didn't come that Wednesday, of course, so all afternoon I had those sacks on my mind. I'd go to the door—yep! Sacks still there. It's raining—go out and move the sacks. Night came—will the sacks be safe? Morning—better check the sacks. On Thursday the men were late in coming, and once again I assumed responsibility for watching over the sacks. Then they came. I watched as the men picked them up—*my* sacks—and drove away with them in the back of their truck. The sacks had changed hands; they were not my burden any longer.

Since that Thursday years ago, I haven't called the Salvation Army a single time to check on those sacks. I suppose you could say I trusted them to take care of the things I gave them and, since they do that kind of work all the time, I was confident it would be done well.

Letting those sacks go is a simple analogy of a profound practice: giving a burden to the Lord and leaving it there. Even when the burden is immense and crushing, the exercise of giving it over to Him, of "casting" it onto Him, is no different.

A Heavy Envelope

Our son was 13 when an orthopedic physician diagnosed his "leg problem" as a rare bone disorder. The future? Bleak. That was in February. In June, he underwent extensive testing at an orthopedic, diagnostic institute; the report came in the mail that week. Bill was in Denver at the time, and I vacillated between wanting to open the letter and fearing to open it alone. I decided to wait.

Saturday was forever in coming, and Bill's plane didn't land until 8:28 in the evening. By the time we got home, sorted through the souvenirs and gifts, and settled the boys down for the night, it was nearly 10:30. Now for the mail.

The letter was written with cool, tactless formality; the test results were just as objective, just as cruel. I couldn't collect my thoughts. I was so discouraged, so crushed and resentful: "God, I don't understand. It seems to me he has all he can manage in life as it is. What's going on? What are You doing?" Futility.

In complete desperation and at 12:15 in the morning, I gave my son to the Lord. I know I did. I have an envelope to prove that I did. It has "June 27, 1976, 12:15 A.M., GOD" written on the outside. The letter is still folded, *inside.*

How many times I've wanted to take him back. From my kitchen window I could see him walking home from school, and I could tell if he was hurting. A heaviness would creep over me, and I would be bombarded with empathetic thoughts of despair and discouragement. But I trained myself to parry with the truth: "Thank You, Lord, that *You* have him; I gave him to You. Minister to him through me, please." Then I'd meet him at the door, talk to him, fix him a peanut butter sandwich, and let him know how much I had missed him through the day.

I have several "problem envelopes," but God has my problems.

What do you do with your burdens? With those circumstances that seem almost incapacitating? You write, you call, you talk with a good friend, you write again, you eat, you sleep, you call again, you think it and breathe it, you live every detail over and over—and it always seems to wind up on your back, right? Or how do you help when people you know are experiencing heartache? When you know the emotional pain must be excruciating? When you see them routinely facing each day and you know that they are longing for relief, for prayers to be answered, for the wrong to be all right again?

We've heard it said that, "Seeing is believing," and though Jesus gently chided Thomas for requiring a touch, a revelation before his eyes, it is that seeing—that *knowing* that we saw—which brings belief home to us and serves as a tangible validation. We can go shopping for a wedding trousseau, we can attend the delightful showers, and we can help pack the suitcase, but until we *see* our daughter walking down the aisle, until we *see* her waving to us from the getaway car—only then does a vague semblance of reality set in: *She's married.*

In the same way, talking about which college to attend and planning the first-semester courses—even writing out the tuition check—don't seem to convince us that "our baby" is leaving home. It's when we try to pack all his personal belongings (including his mountain bike) into his VW and *watch* him drive off toward college that our eyes begin to tear and this strange realization blankets us: The nest is empty. Seeing helps us to believe, to acknowledge the truth and then pack up the remnants and start again.

At this moment you may be enduring a difficult and painful experience in your life; you may be dealing with someone over whom you have no control. It may have started just recently, or it could be the lingering stigma of an incident from your past. You want desperately to give this burden to God, to know that He has it in His hands; you want release from the stress, the depression, the pressure, the pain, the weariness. The following is a seeing-is-believing exercise for giving a burden to the Lord—and *leaving it there.*

1. Get a watch, a felt-tipped pen, a piece of paper, a pencil, an envelope, and a half brick (or something around the same weight and size).
2. Go to the nearest store that carries helium balloons and buy a plump one.
3. With all your paraphernalia, go to a field, a

vacant lot, the football stadium, the park—anywhere spacious without trees or buildings.

4. With your felt-tipped pen, write as many details of your circumstance as you need to on the balloon in order to identify it with your problems.

5. Now, hold your brick and the string to the balloon in your hand, lifting your arm straight out in front of you. As you do this, begin talking to the Lord about your burden; tell Him every detail! Tell Him you can't carry this burden any longer; tell Him how angry you are, how hurt, how tired—tell Him *everything*. Hold that brick and balloon up until your arm is hurting so badly you don't know if you're crying over your burden or because of the pain in your arm.

6. When you can't hold your arm up another second, with the command for "casting your burden on the Lord" in your heart and mind, praying and thanking Him for His concern, His power, and His love for you, *drop the brick and set your balloon free*, releasing your burden and easing your pain. Watch it climb, see it disappear into the very dwelling place of God.

7. Finally, take your paper and record the date and time with this statement: "On _____ (date), at _____ (time), I gave my burden to the Lord." Now print this: "And He took it." Look for the balloon. Can you see it? A tiny speck?

    Fold your paper and put it in your envelope. Seal it and print "God" and the date and time on the front. Don't lose that envelope; you will pick it up many times and thank God for what He did for you on this day.

8. Thank Him. When you get home, get three index cards and write GOD/the date/the time on each one. Put those cards someplace where you will see them often (over the sink, in the medicine cabinet, on the dash of your car). Every time you glance at a card, visualize that speck in the sky—the burden, out of your control and in the arms of God.

It's a simple exercise, and yet it will be much like an altar erected in remembrance, reminding you of what God has done. Does this mean you will never cry again? No. Does it mean your emotions will never rocket to the top again? Of course not. Will you want desperately to take the burden back at times? Yes. Does this mean that you will not hurt anymore or that you are not to be involved in that person's life anymore? No. You continue to encourage him, to minister to him; you communicate with him, tell him what you think and feel. There has been only one decisive change: *The burden is no longer yours.*

When you give God your burden, when you cast it onto Him, He picks up the sacks—*your sacks*—and drives off with them. Do you suppose you can trust Him to take care of the burden you gave Him? Yes, and you can be confident it will be done well, beyond your wildest imaginings, really—He does this kind of work all the time.

Dear Anabel,

This past Tuesday my husband and I purchased two helium balloons (one pink, one blue), then drove up into the mountains. We found a good lookout point and parked. We both sat for a long time, writing all over our balloons. Al didn't read what I wrote, and I didn't read what he wrote.

I was the first to let mine go. The wind was blowing odd, sort of down into the valley. The balloon tangled in the tree branches, blew loose, and after the third tree, broke wildly toward the sky!

Then Al let his balloon go—in a different spot to avoid the trees—but one got his, too. I walked over to the tree, put both hands on the trunk and shook it. The balloon caught the wind and took off toward the heavens.

That's a good picture of what this circumstance has been for us, Anabel—a real struggle to let it go, to make it fly.

I "feel" more free than I have felt in years, and when the negative thoughts do come, I close my eyes and see those pink and blue balloons going and going . . . and I know it's all right, Anabel.

God has everything in His hands.

Will You Go With Me?

It was Monday morning when the call came.
"Anabel, this is Dianne. Do you remember me?"
"Of course, I do. How are you?"
"Do you have just a few minutes to talk?"
"Yes."
"Ron and I have been married for 20 years," she began, "and it's been a good marriage. At times he wasn't as close to the Lord as I would have liked him to be, but I gave that to Him. You may remember that Ron travels.

He leaves the house on Monday morning and doesn't get home until Thursday evening. I know that's not good, but we've made the best of it, and he's always attentive to me and the children over the weekend."

She continued, "About a year ago, he rededicated his life to the Lord, and everything has been just wonderful since then. He has done so well. There was something that seemed to be bothering him, but I was so happy, I wasn't about to make any waves."

At this point, Dianne lost her composure, began crying, and with difficulty told the rest of her story.

"Last night, when we got home from church, Ron said he wanted to talk with me. So we got the kids in bed and then sat down at the kitchen table together." There was a pause. "Oh, Anabel, this is so hard for me to say. Ron confessed to me that over the past 20 years he has had relationships with several women . . . in some towns, the same woman every time he was there. It was amazing to me—the calmness I felt. I assured Ron that I understood, that I forgave him, and that everything was going to be all right. And, Anabel, last night it was. But when he drove away this morning, I collapsed and it isn't all right at all. I'm a basket case. I've got to have help. . . ."

I gave Dianne the instructions for giving a burden to the Lord and suggested that she should do it today—while Ron was gone and while the hurt was so heavy. It was just a week later that I received this letter from her:

Dear Anabel,

I went to the lake that afternoon, armed with my paper, my pencil, my watch, my envelope, and my big silver balloon, and I did what you told me to do.

You cannot imagine the relief that came over me. It has been so beautiful, so wonderful. It's all right, Anabel, it's really *all right.*

But that's not the most exciting thing. When Ron came home Thursday night, he could tell that I was free . . . truly free, so he asked, "Dianne, tell me about it. What's happened?"

So we sat down, and I told him what I had done. When I finished, he thought for a moment, and then he said to me, "Di, will you go with me to buy a balloon?"

9

Putting Asunder

Work was everything to a generation that knew the struggles of unemployment. Family is everything to a generation that knows the suffering of divorce.

—Alan Deuschman

Each divorce is the death of a small civilization.

—Pat Conroy

Pam's mother had been an excellent cook. Now that Mom was gone, Pam inherited all the delicious recipes that everyone loved—especially that elegant chocolate dessert. But Pam had tried now to make it four times. Something obviously was not right.

One day Pam was looking through an old church cookbook with recipes submitted by the members. There it was! Mom's chocolate dessert. *Is there a difference between this recipe and mine?* she wondered, carefully reading over the instructions in the cookbook. *Well, can you beat that! No wonder I was failing.* And sure enough, the next try was a roaring success.

Pam couldn't make her mom's dessert right because she didn't know what she was doing wrong.

Could this be our problem with marriage today? How can we "make it right" when we "don't know what we're doing wrong"?

Women who have experienced the trauma of divorce know that their "recipe" lacked something. Single women are poring through all sorts of recipe books, having made up their minds that when they try they want to do it right. Some married women are "borrowing recipes" like crazy. They're sick of eating inedible delicacies.

Marriage. Home. Family. Security. Love. Happiness. They all seem so illusive. And why do we cling to the old song that haunts our houses every Christmas: *I'll be home for Christmas, you can count on me . . . ?* Because deep within, planted there by God Himself, is the desire, the need, the longing for home.

Yet something is wrong with our recipe. Divorce is rampant. The single-again population is experiencing meteoric growth. Single-parent children are the norm. Our world is frantically searching for love, security . . . for *home.*

Don't Throw Away—May Come Back in Style

From the fairy-tale ending, "And they lived happily ever after," to the casual commitment with which we walk down the aisle thinking, *If it doesn't work out, we can always get a divorce,* our concepts of and our attitudes toward marriage today are grotesquely warped. We live like roommates, stitched together with thin strands called *children, convenience, social status, reputation,* or *security.* In his book, *The Closing of the American Mind,* Allan Bloom, professor of social thought at Chicago University, writes:

> When marriage occurs, it does not usually seem to result from a decision and a conscious will to take on its responsibilities. The couple have lived together for a long time, and by an almost imperceptible process, they find themselves married, as much out of convenience as passion, as much negatively as positively (not really expecting to do much better, since they have looked around and seen how imperfect all fits seem to be).

How sad. It seems as though the biblical concept of marriage has become archaic and outmoded, or like an old computer, outdated. We put it in a box, stash it in the attic, and label it, "Don't Throw Away—May Come Back in Style." And downstairs, where we live and move through the house, we have become separate entities far more apart than together. Oneness? Unity? Commitment? Integrity? Love? These words define marriage? Hardly.

Is it such a wonder, then, that today's young people want to "try out" their mate *before* they get married? They aren't fools! They want no part of anything that faintly resembles the "blissful state of matrimony" their mom and dad exemplified. Hell couldn't be *much* worse than home—cold indifference, emotional tension, abuse, insecurity, hostility, materialism, the I-me-mine philosophy, bitter words deliberately designed to hurt, the total absence of love. Others have lived through the trauma of seeing their parents call it quits and then having to choose Mom or Dad, with visiting privileges for the loser.

Home. What a travesty, what a fraud! So much of what we know of love and marriage we learn at home, and that is why *marriage* has a new definition today: "a write-off; a great chance at making a gross mistake; a concept or way of life that should, for the most part, be avoided; a fearful proposition."

"If living together for a couple of years out of wedlock can save me from a lifetime of hell on earth, I'm ready. I don't want to go through what my parents went through."

"If sex can satisfy this need, this hunger, then why should it matter how I get it or who I get it from? Why should I tie myself to one person for life?"

"I enjoy the 'single life.' My time is my own; my paycheck doesn't cover anyone's liabilities but my own; I do whatever I want to do. Marriage would box me in and give me responsibilities that I'm not interested in accepting. Besides, there's such a risk in getting married. You can be hurt, and I don't want that. I can satisfy my sexual needs when they get 'too hot to handle.' I know that's not what God intended—but I'm just being honest."

So her needs are met: to be held, loved, and accepted; to hear words, tender and gentle; to be touched, to feel special (and this may be for 30 minutes, or two weeks, or two months). And his needs are met: to feel masculine and satisfied; to feel needed and loved; to be praised.

But that isn't the answer, is it? Isn't there a plan? Isn't there a key? Is marriage, is love, something to be endured? Is it all outdated and too small to wear? *Where do we turn?*

Let marriage be held in honor (esteemed worthy, precious, [that is,] of great price, and especially dear) in all things (Hebrews 13:4, AMP).

For this reason a man shall leave his father and mother and shall be united firmly (joined inseparably) to his wife, and the two shall become one flesh? So they are no longer two, but one flesh. What therefore God has joined together, let not man put asunder (separate) (Matthew 19:5,6, AMP).

"Joined inseparably."

"The two shall become one."

Isn't this what we all long for? Isn't this the dream we cling to?

And dreams do come true. Rarely overnight, though. They take time and work. Lots of hard work. And that can be so discouraging. Thoughts begin to come: *I can't go on. Give up. How much longer can I endure this? Give up. There's absolutely no hope. Give up. I've done everything I know to do. Give up. Give up. Give up.* Until finally, we give up. All we want is out! It seems to be our only escape route, the only way to make the hurt go away, to stop the arguments and the angry words, the depression, the crying, the lonely nights that seem to never end.

From the dream of being "joined inseparably" to the nightmare of being "put asunder."

Asunder/Divorce. Into pieces/Divorce. Fragmented/Divorce. Different directions/Divorce.

I wonder: Have we convinced ourselves that because divorce happens so often . . . it's easy . . . "no fault" . . . painless?

Before we examine "joined inseparably," I want us to examine "put asunder." Painful? Probably. Profitable? Definitely.

If you have been through a divorce, I wish I could put my arms around you and let you know I care. I don't want to hurt you.

If you're contemplating divorce, I pray that you will be very open to what you read. Know, dear one, exactly what you are contemplating.

If you're the child of divorced parents, you'll find yourself in these words. And you will understand.

Once Upon a Time

His name was Oreo, and he had lived in the neighborhood all his life. Everyone knew him and loved him. But then something tragic happened to Oreo: The people he lived with decided to get a divorce, the man going one way and the woman another, abandoning the home he had always known. Now, moving just wasn't Oreo's thing, so he decided not to be "codependent" any longer and stayed behind, all by himself.

He changed over the weeks and months. No one could talk to him or even come close to him anymore. The neighbors fixed food and put it out regularly, and it disappeared. But if they ever happened out when he was there, he'd leave the much-needed food and head for safety and security—in dark places, smelly places, frightening places, places he would never have gone if "home" were still there.

Oreo was a cat . . . a little, scared, brown and white cat who just couldn't handle divorce.

Once upon a time, we were all confident (that *is* the beginning of a fairy tale, isn't it?). But that's not unusual. There has never been a "just married" couple who, while snuggled down in the warmth and passion of each other's arms in the honeymoon hotel, had this conversation:

"Let's give it our best for three or four years, Honey," she says. "And then I'll start being real bossy and you'll start being real hateful, okay?"

"Okay," he agrees. "And then about eight years along, why don't I start seeing some other woman, because by then you'll have become disenchanted with our love life (since I'm being so nasty) and won't be the sweet, responsive lover you are now. Sound good?"

"Well, I guess so. And then, of course, I'll get depressed and unhappy. . . ."

That's ridiculous, isn't it? So what *does* happen? If we're so determined to make our marriages work, why do half of them fail? Are we oblivious to the dangers that can wreak such havoc in a relationship? Do we get blindsided by them? Are we so self-centered that we don't care what happens to the person we at one time loved enough to say, "I want to spend the rest of my life loving you"? Or are we simply flippant toward our commitment in marriage, toward marriage itself? How have we become so casual about the death rate of marriage?

If "every divorce is the death of a small civilization," then we can understand why we're surrounded by lifeless, lonely, disillusioned, driven people.

Dr. Judith Wallerstein is the founder and executive director of the Center for the Family in Transition in Corte Madera, California, which counsels more divorcing families than any other agency in America. Her book, *Second Chances* (Ticknor and Fields, 1989), is the only ten-year longitudinal study of divorce. It should be mandatory reading for premarital and pre-divorce counseling. As the dust-jacket copy reveals, it is a "landmark work that may forever change the way we think about marriage, the family, and our moral commitments to our spouses and children."

Dr. Wallerstein's years of research dissolve the tiniest notions of the easy-divorce myth. (The term *easy* may apply to the ease of *obtaining* a divorce these days, but it certainly does not apply to the *results* of divorce.) You cannot casually scan the pages of *Second Chances* as though you were leafing through your new, spring sale catalog. You see the victims, you hear their words and feel their despair, you are aghast at their shattered lives and wonder what's going to happen to the very foundation of our civilization: home.

We hold in such esteem the individual's *rights* and *opinions* that we hesitate to take issue on almost every subject. After all, you have your right to your own opinion, and what right do I have to infringe on your personal code of ethics? I'm going to use Dr. Wallerstein's findings in an effort to do just that—influence the way you think about divorce, to give you reason to consider divorce very carefully.

The following material, compiled from both Dr. Wallerstein's experience and my own, consists of general *opinions* concerning divorce as compared and contrasted with the indisputable *facts* about divorce and poignant testimonies documenting its sad *results*.

> **Opinion:** I know it will be difficult for my daughter, but it's going to be difficult for all of us. She's young . . . she'll get over it.

Fact: "Divorce is likely to be the greatest stress [a child] will face while growing up" (*Second Chances*, p. xv).

Result: It's Christmas Eve; tomorrow all the children will be sitting around the table, and there will be a lot of kidding and laughter. But I know them so well.

I look into their eyes and there's sadness. "Dad isn't here. . . ." They still can't believe that he walked away from them and never looked back to see if they were crying.

Opinion: Kids are different in our day and time. Things like divorce just don't affect them. A majority of their friends have gone through the same thing, so they aren't alone.

Fact: "Divorce is a different experience for children and adults because the children lose something that is fundamental to their development—the family structure" (*Second Chances*, p. 11).

Result: "If you had three wishes, Sammy, what would they be?"

"I wish [my parents] would get back together. That's wish one, two, and three." Bursting into tears, he said, "That's all I want" (*Second Chances*, p. 73).

"[My parents] didn't understand anything," Steve says. "It's like I wasn't a person. It was like I didn't have feelings" (*Second Chances*, p. 147).

Opinion: Self-actualization is what is important today, and if I stay in this relationship, my children are not going to learn from my example how to survive.

I have a right to my own life just as surely as they have a right to theirs.

Fact: "The changing roles of men and women, greater sexual freedom, and the high rate of divorce make courtship riskier. Adolescents feel the effects of these changes in society, and they are afraid of rejection, failure, and disappointment. . . . They fear betrayal. They fear abandonment. They fear loss.

"They draw an inescapable conclusion: Relationships have a high likelihood of being untrustworthy; betrayal and infidelity are probable. . . . To become an adult . . . one must be able to seek out and establish an intimate and committed relationship. It helps enormously to have imprinted on one's emotional circuitry the patterning of a successful, enduring relationship between a man and a woman. . . . It is parents who carve the deepest impressions on children" (*Second Chances*, p. 55).

Result: I guess you finally just decide to stop hurting. I understand why my parents divorced. They were never happy. All they did was argue and fight.

They were so busy fighting with each other they never seemed to notice me . . .

or to care what was happening in my life. I'm afraid to get too close to a boy. Oh, sex is okay, but there's too great a risk involved in expecting him to commit himself to me. I don't want what my parents had, and they never intended for it to end like this. Don't expect things and then you don't get hurt.

Opinion: We made the decision together. Goodness knows I've tried to make it work. It just seems that we never could get on the same track in any area of our lives. I thought I loved him, and he thought he loved me. We'll both be better off starting all over again . . . probably.

Fact: "The true measure of divorce is found long after the shouting stops and the lawyers go home; it is calibrated according to how people feel about themselves years later, how their lives have changed, for better or worse" (*Second Chances*, p. 28).

Result: I still question my being desirable as a female, and I've been divorced over ten years.

I was getting dressed one morning and realized I had been wearing the same pair of trousers for the last two weeks. Nothing seems important anymore.

Single Again

The fastest growing group of adults in our churches today is not expanding because we have parties and invite them to come, nor is it growing via a well-organized visitation program. It's a group whose members congregate because of a shared tragedy, a group that is unique in its entry requirement: *You must suffer to be eligible.* If the emotional pain experienced by these millions of people could be heard, the sound would be deafening! There are enough broken hearts and splintered dreams, enough hours of life spent in varied degrees of despair and agony, to cause anyone to fall into a limp heap on the floor and moan, "I can't go on." I'm talking about that group we call, very poignantly, *single again.*

I was speaking to a group of women in Springfield, Missouri, and wanted to find out where they were in their marriage relationships, so I asked them to let me know this way: "Everyone close your eyes and hold up your right hand. Now, a clenched fist means your marriage is bad, and five fingers means it's super. On a scale of none to five, rate your marriage for me." About a year later I received a letter from one of those women. She wrote this: "I held up five fingers that day, Anabel. My marriage was super, or so I thought. Six months later my husband informed me that there was another woman competing for my place in his life—she had been for quite some time—and that the game was over and I was the loser. You never could have convinced me, when you were here, that I would one day wear that label, 'single again.'"

I have talked and wept with hundreds of women experiencing the agony of divorce; watching as the chintz curtains were boxed and the pansy bed was trampled; trying to decide to whom the little things they had bought with their husbands should go (trying not to remember the fun it had been bringing home the trinkets and finding just the right place to display them); hearing, as though through water, the cry of their first child and wondering what to do with the photograph albums; knowing that the fireplace would not be lighted again on cool, fall evenings—that like their dreams, the hearth was cold and lifeless.

Effective Examples

Dr. Wallerstein writes, "It helps enormously to have imprinted on one's emotional circuitry the patterning of a successful, enduring relationship between a man and a woman" (*Second Chances*, p. 55). "Imprinted on one's emotional circuitry"—that imprinting is the programming we identified and discussed in Chapter 4. The child whose parents exemplify that "successful, enduring relationship" is secure in being loved and can leave her mother and daddy sitting on the divan to go outside and play. But if she does not have that example, if her parents separate or are not "successful," stamping her with insecurity, she's afraid to leave them, fearing that her "love objects" might disappear.

Security, which is one of the effects of love, determines how I view my world as a young adult, and this security—or lack of security—is a direct result of my interaction with the people in my early, private world, that unique childhood environment. (We're back to the beginning, talking about patterns burned into our memory banks—techniques we revert to, having built them as we grew up, striving for love and acceptance. We're back to our unique version of the flesh, but *we do not have to be controlled by these patterns any longer!* We are not irreparable. We have been set free! We are new!)

Furthermore, our desire to enter into an intimate

relationship, *wholly committed to making it work*, is constructed brick by brick, day after day, year by year, as we live with parents who demonstrate that commitment, who maintain that type of relationship while acting their roles, their "give and take" infused with integrity. And what happens when the role models are faulty? Bad things. Any number of imprints, or programs, can scar us, and, since we learn by example, the tragedy often repeats itself.

There are millions who could testify to such tragedy. Many of you reading this book have written pages of heartbreak and pain in your journal, struggling for understanding; fighting self-condemnation, bitterness, fear, and disillusionment; feeling used, having seen years of your life wadded up and trashed, an unwilling victim—a child numbly wandering through the tragic drama of divorce. Perhaps the pain and memories are buried, but somehow, somewhere, sometime, it all surfaces:

> [The adult children of divorce] seem propelled by despair and anxiety as they search for what they fear they will never find. They abhor cheating yet find themselves in multiple relationships that lead to cheating. They want marriage but are terrified of it. They detest divorce but end up divorced. They believe in love but expect to be betrayed. Such grave inconsistencies make life difficult (*Second Chances*, p. 56).

My dear one, with these inconsistencies, with this sparse *commitment* to certain standards, anything can happen. A sense of restlessness, confusion, or lack of concern for *any* values will permeate every thought, every act.

Who you are is all wrapped up in what you believe: "What *do* I believe? I used to think divorce was wrong. Now, I'm not sure. I'd like to be made out of steel, but I feel like I'm made out of plastic. Tell me about *your* system of deciding what's wrong and right. Oh, you're confused, too? You don't have a system either? Then what's to keep us from doing anything, everything?"

This lack of commitment, this lack of integrity, is the root of the problem: "If it doesn't work out, we can always get a divorce. After all, Mom and Dad did." We don't really *expect* an until-death-do-us-part marriage; we don't *commit* ourselves to one person. Perhaps we are confident in *our* ability to make it work: "I'll give marriage a whirl. No harm done; I can do it." But when a marriage fails, when love dies, the results are far-reaching and disastrous.

Light

The night has a thousand eyes,
    And the day but one;
Yet the light of the bright world dies,
    With the dying sun.

The mind has a thousand eyes,
    And the heart but one;
Yet the light of a whole life dies,
    When love is done.

—Francis W. Bourdillion

I pray that you will ask God to renew your commitment to the sanctity of marriage. I pray that you will offer yourself as a healing agent, as the vessel that God can use to turn ashes into beauty, as the one who commits herself to being "all God created me to be." But you must remember—*you cannot do it,* but there is Someone living inside you, giving you great confidence as you dare to enter the precarious realm of marriage.

This is not an easy walk, and certainly not one that I would have chosen, but it is what lies in front of me, and it cannot be diverted. I am not after a divorce, and I am not looking for a man out there who would treat me decently, who would love me and respect me. I made a vow before God to be true to this man until "death parts us," and I am committed to see this through. In a very literal sense, I feel that I am being stripped of depending on anyone but Jesus. That's all right, Anabel, He will never divorce me.

Oreo Can Be Salvaged . . .

I was the only one who came to Hulen Tower II for work this morning; it's kind of spooky being all by myself in this huge building. As I walked up the steps, there was a cat sitting at the door, looking in. I stopped, but he heard me and turned, every muscle tense, frightened, and ready to fight for his life. What a mess he was: fur all matted and sores everywhere, ear torn, skin and bones.

Oreo can be salvaged. Someone will have to come into his life who isn't afraid of getting scratched or dirty, who won't hesitate to rummage through the garbage pails or crawl under the house to find him—a kitty cat whose heart is beating like crazy but who's trying to act awfully tough. And that someone will have to spend time waiting for Oreo to come to the food dish; they'll have to be there. Oreo will gradually get used to the presence and won't be so afraid. Trust will come slowly, but it will come. One day, that someone will actually be able to hold that furry, little brown and white creature, bring him in to where he had been before he left, and touch where it hurts with love.

"Here kitty, kitty." I knelt. "Will you let me pet you? I'll take you home with me. I'll clean you up and feed you. You'd be warm there, and you'd have a basket to sleep in— or you could sleep on my lap. And you wouldn't have to hide in the woods or fight dogs anymore either. I'll take good care of you. Oh, don't run away. I promise I won't hurt you. I only want to love you. Here kitty, kitty . . ."

10

Created as One

This was God's original plan before the tragic fall—man and woman created as one, designed to function as one, and completely dependent on one another for fulfilling their God-ordained roles.

Adam threw back his head and laughed with delight! The beauty of Eden surrounded him. Animals grazed contentedly; songs came from all directions—the birds, the brooks, the breeze.

And God had created woman! Eve. How grateful he was to God for giving him something so beautiful. No. Eve wasn't a "some-thing"; she was a "some-one." Every day had been a wonderful experience in the Garden, but since Eve had come—how could he explain it? Before Eve, he hadn't realized—to touch, to talk, to be with her. Yes, life was good.

His step quickened as he saw her sitting by the tree in the center of the Garden, and for a moment he stood quietly, loving and watching. She wasn't aware of his presence; she seemed to be deep in thought, as though she might be—troubled?

"Eve, I wish you could see your hair," he said as he approached. "Every strand is gold in the sun. How beautiful you are. Do you have any idea how much I love you?"

"Yes, Adam, I know, I know," she brushed his comment aside. "Adam, I did something terrible today, something I shouldn't have done. Don't be angry with me. I don't know why I did it."

"It can't be that bad. Let's go talk to God about it."

"Oh, no, I've got to talk to you alone. How foolish of me! Help me, Adam. I need you."

He had never known such emotions. He had never seen Eve distressed like this, crying to him for help. He held her. "You don't need to be afraid. I'm here with you, and I won't go anywhere. Tell me about it. What happened?"

His hold didn't loosen as Eve, sobbing, told him about the events of the day; no, it became tighter and he held her closer. He didn't hear everything because the words God had said began coming back to him. Was it just yesterday? "In the day that you eat of that tree, you will die."

His mind raced: What has happened? This can't be true! Eve, what have you done? If she dies, then I'll be alone again. Life without Eve? To touch, to talk, to be with her? To have no one but God?

"Adam, you won't leave me, will you?"

The Definition of a Woman

I don't know that the distinction of being a woman has ever been so widely read about, written about, disputed, pondered, and legislated as it is today, or if in any previous period of history woman has been so maligned, militant, insecure, confused, or discontent. Opinions bombard us:

"Any simpleton can keep house, no qualifications or training required—just a good, strong back."

"Any woman can satisfy a man's sexual needs; it will also profit both parties to maintain a 'sexual smorgasbord' of partners."

"I have every right to enjoy a satisfying career! I'm destroying myself buried at home, changing diapers, wiping runny noses, limiting my vocabulary to two-year-old jabber."

"A daycare center fulfills the needs of a child, provides her with a broader education, causes her to be more socially secure."

What has been lost in this age of radical change, in this era of "awakening," is God's definition of woman: competent, trustworthy, strong, faithful, energetic, sensitive, confident, well-organized, intelligent, industrious, creative, compassionate, respected, wise, resourceful, gracious, poised, secure, gentle, kind, courageous . . . (Proverbs 31). *I choose God's adjectives; after all, He is the one who made me.*

Yes, God created man, woman, and marriage. Marriage: A male and female, entirely unique, agreeing to join themselves together with vows of love, commitment, and trust; two facing life as one, realizing that love will not hold their marriage together, but that their marriage will hold their love together; acknowledging each other's imperfections, but accepting each other nonetheless; loving each other enough to change, enough to understand, be patient, and not inflict pain—for better, for worse; for richer, for poorer; in sickness and in health until, through death, they attain perfection and come to know each other as they have never known before.

He: "I will protect you."
She: "I will encourage you."
He: "I will provide for you."
She: "I will be your partner."
He: "I will walk with you."
She: "I will hold your hand."
He: "I will never leave you."
She: "I will love you."

In His Beginning

Do you remember the story of creation? God did well! After every undertaking He sat back, viewed His handiwork, and said, "Yes, that's good." And then He created Adam. When He had finished that chore, He sat back, looked at him, and said, "This is *not* good. It isn't right that man should be alone. I'm going to create another being in *my* image as a helper for him, to complete him" (see Genesis 2:18). So God created Eve, completing His original creation. Then He formally commissioned them: "Be fruitful and multiply" (Genesis 1:28). It was a commission neither of them was capable of carrying out alone.

God created them male and female, but He created them as *one:* "He created them male and female, and He blessed *them* and *named them Man* in the day when they were created" (Genesis 5:2, emphasis added). God originally named both the male and the female "man" (*adam* is the Hebrew word for *man*); there was a male-man and a female-man. There was no favoritism, no superiority—one was not standing in front of the other. God gave the marching orders to *them*, not to *him*. The word "woman" was *Adam's* idea: "This is bone of my bones and flesh of my flesh, I'll call her woman." (see Genesis 2:23). He named all the other creatures, why not me? And yet, there was no hierarchy; the male in his *aloneness* was the only facet of creation upon which God looked with dissatisfaction. When God closed shop after the female was formed, He looked upon the two of them together and said, "Now, this is very good" (see Genesis 1:31).

This was God's original plan before the tragic fall—man and woman created as one, designed to function as one, and completely dependent on one another for fulfilling their God-ordained roles.

Now let's stop right here and clarify something: *The single person is not incomplete.* Paul writes, "And in Him you have been made complete" (Colossians 2:10a)—a stipulation of the New Covenant. Your relationship with Christ is a highly individual, very personal, and unique relationship. It does not depend on any other human person for fulfillment. You are complete the moment you accept Jesus Christ into your life as your Lord, your Savior, and your Life. He is your Husband. The Man in your life. Your Companion. Your "Completer." You are "complete *in Him,*" and you will never again be *incomplete.*

When I go to Him of my own free will and say to Him (usually with great joy and expectation), "I have decided I want to be a wife," I am given a new script, a new set of standards. But I am not suddenly "incomplete." The covenant hasn't become null and void. I have simply chosen the role of completer in someone else's life.

In God's genesis, man and woman were to have fellowship with their Creator. They were to experience the peace and the beauty of Eden.

Of all the reasons for the death of our Lord, one stands out with singular clarity: to restore God's creation—Man (male and female)—to the fellowship with Him that he once knew; to establish once more His original plan; to bring Man unto Himself, pure, sinless, and thriving—contented—in the very presence of God Himself, yet unafraid. Naked, yet unashamed. Knowing and being known completely.

Is this relationship with God available to us? Yes! Are we forever cursed? Oh, no. It is true that Adam and Eve's *disobedience* caused us to be sinners separated from God, *but Christ's obedience has made us acceptable to God again:*

> So then as through one transgression [Adam's sin] there resulted condemnation to all men, even so through one act of righteousness [Jesus' death and resurrection] there resulted justification of life to all men. For as through the one man's [Adam] disobedience the many were made sinners, even so through the obedience of the One [Jesus] the many will be made righteous (Romans 5:18,19).

What Adam and Eve did, and the result of what they did, has been canceled, obliterated, and made null and void by the *new* Adam, Jesus (Colossians 2:13,14). His wounds have healed our wounds. We have a new Adam, and just as the first Adam's trespass led to condemnation, the new Adam's obedience leads us to righteousness, life, and freedom. Our physical birth identified us with the first Adam (birth determines identity, right?).

It placed us in bondage, under the curse of God, and brought death—we were spiritual stillbirths. But our *rebirth* (spiritual, Romans 10:9), our union, with the second Adam, Jesus, has set us free! Remember? Our whole history changed. We tasted death *with Him* when He was crucified (Galatians 2:20), and because of Him, all the bonds, debts, and curses that were once ours were erased. So you see, *death truly does set us free* (Romans 6:7).

The first couple were innocent, unstained beings in an unstained world, and though we might experience with our husband in part the beauty of the relationship which Adam and Eve knew, we will never know the complete freedom, oneness, joy, and beauty that was theirs. Oh, the peace of Eden is beyond our grasp. Our peace comes from the Garden of Gethsemane.

The Completion of a Man

So man and woman are unique—two and yet, when joined in marriage, one. In order for two separate identities to become one and still retain their uniqueness, they must *complete* one another, each filling the void left by the other, completing the space the other can't fill. Two identical puzzle pieces won't fit together and make one; you could superimpose one over the other, but then the second piece would lose its identity behind the first.

This is not God's plan, but you have undoubtedly seen marriages like it: You look directly into the eyes of the husband, address him by name, ask him a personal question about himself, and the answer promptly comes from the mouth of his wife. (He probably even walks a respectful three paces behind her when they shop for his clothing!) Or you have encountered the wife who has learned, through whatever channels of abuse, that there is only one *acceptable* response to her husband: "Whatever you say, Dear."

No, that is *not* acceptable! That is *not* God's plan! God created *two* individuals, and for the two to become one, they must complete each other and yet maintain their individuality. They must complement each other. (*Complement:* to fill up or complete; that which is required to supply a deficiency; one or two mutually completing parts.) Look at Genesis 2:18:

> And the Lord God said, "It isn't good for man to be alone; I will make a companion for him, a helper suited to his needs" (TLB).

> Then the Lord God said, "It is not good for the man to be alone; I will make a helper suitable for him" (NASB).

> Now the Lord God said, It is not good (sufficient, satisfactory) that the man should be alone; I will make him a helper meet (suitable, adapted, completing) for him (AMP).

> Then the Lord God said, "It is not good that the man should be alone; I will make him a helper fit for him" (RSV).

Each of the above translations uses the word *helper*, meaning "one who helps." You don't help a person by doing *for* him what he is capable of doing himself—that would cripple him, it would take away his motivation and his purpose. The Living Bible says that God gave Adam "a helper suited to his needs." You don't meet a man's needs by giving him something he already has. The Amplified Version, providing alternate translations for *helper*, uses the word *completing*. You do not complete a man by duplicating him—God did not create Jimmy and Johnny; He created Jimmy and Jane. You meet a man's needs—you *complete* him—by providing what is missing, what is lacking or necessary. Using the church as a model, Paul explained this *completion* in his first letter to the Corinthians:

> So God has put the body [the church] together in such a way that extra honor and care are given to those parts that might otherwise seem less important. This makes for happiness among the parts, so that the parts have the same care for each other that they do for themselves. If one part suffers, all parts suffer with it, and if one part is honored, all the parts are glad (12:24-26, TLB).

Again, in Romans 12:4,5, Paul writes:

> Just as there are many parts to our bodies, so it is with Christ's body. We are all parts of it, and it takes every one of us to make it complete, for we each have different work to do. So we belong to each other, and each needs all the others (TLB).

Individually, we are parts of one another, and it is not that one is more important than the other in this male and female classification—it is only as they are together that they are complete: "However, in the Lord, neither is woman independent of man, nor is man independent of woman" (1 Corinthians 11:11). Man and woman were designed to depend on each other. Their very *existence* is inherent in each other, and it is only as they are *one* that they achieve God's plan, that they experience the beauty He has designed for them in their marriage.

11

If two lives join, there is oft a scar. They are one and one, with a shadowy third; One near one is too far. . . .

—Robert Browning

One of the most tender and intimate moments I remember with my dad occurred while we were sitting out on the back porch step one evening. I was sitting between his legs, and he had his arms around my neck. My mother had just undergone a hysterectomy. I didn't understand Dad's words when he said to me, "You know, Honey, you're the only little boy I'll ever have."

I can't remember being a tomboy specifically for Dad, but I was a super-duper tomboy. The neighborhood kids gathered in our backyard, and there were always boys in the group. That didn't matter to me. If we played cowboys and Indians, I was the chief. If we played cops and robbers, I was the head honcho, be it the sheriff or the "godfather." I even remember Dad tying ropes in the mulberry tree so I could be Tarzan.

Then there were the races down "under the hill" during recess in the sixth grade. (I've since been back to survey the "hill"; it's about three feet high.) I always won. My two greatest victories were when I beat Mervin McConnell and Joe Harold West. I reveled in defeating Joe Harold; he was my boyfriend.

Another red-letter day was the annual trek up Cavanaugh Mountain. I had a crush on Robert Henry Kendrick. How was I going to get him to notice me? Why, the same way I had been getting boys to notice me ever since the backyard get-togethers and races down under the hill: I'll do whatever he does as well as he does—or even better. And I did.

When we started up the mountain, Robert Henry was the leader of the pack, but I was right by his side all the way to the top. I can still remember the thrill of sitting with him on the big, flat rock looking over the Poteau River Valley, waiting for the others to catch up with us. He noticed me! He said something like, "You're quite a mountain climber, Anabel." My heart sang, but my joy was short-lived. He *carried* Joan Caldwell down the mountain because she had a blister on her foot! (Sigh)

About this time I became aware of something in the movies: Humphrey Bogart and Lauren Bacall. Nice. Then I saw *Mrs. Miniver* with Greer Garson and Walter Pidgeon, and I liked what I saw—a marriage where two people had fun together, respected each other, and loved each other deeply. I began to think, *Maybe being a girl isn't all that bad.* Some people would identify this change as "cultural conditioning"; I call it "Creationist's conception." I was beginning to discover what God had created me to be: something beautiful, something special . . . a female.

Marriage—His Creation and Definition

Did God have any idea how hard it would be for the two to become "one flesh"? Did He know just how different we were going to be? How we would have to struggle with this oneness? Yes. Remember that He made us. Uniquely female. Uniquely male. But He didn't tell us to become one and, with some parting words of encouragement, leave us on our own: "You all be careful now, you hear?" Thumb back through the pages you've read. We are *instructed Christians.* So with great excitement we say, "What do you mean, Lord? How do we become one? I really want to know, even though it seems unattainable. Show me. I'm willing, I'm ready, and I'm completely able—for You, Lord, will perform through me."

I read an article recently by the feminist author and activist Vivian Gornick, in which she wrote, "The two shall be as one is over, no matter how lonely we get."[1] How terribly sad. God intends for the exact opposite to take place: He wants us, as husband and wife, to become one in every way—*spiritually, physically, perceptually,* and *emotionally.* He wants to incorporate into our marriage all the intricate details for which the plan calls. He wants our marriage to be everything He intended for it to be (see Figure 11.1 and Figure 11.2).

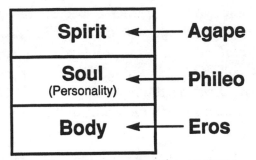

There are three areas of love where we are to become one:
Agape (spirit), **Phileo** (soul), and **Eros** (body or physical).

Figure 11.1

In *Second Chances,* Dr. Judith Wallerstein makes this observation:

> A sense of "we-ness" emerges out of a stable marriage, as each person identifies with some other person's values and attitudes. . . . As the years go by, these identifications strengthen and a new marital identity is formed. As it becomes difficult for one or both partners to think of themselves outside the context of the marriage, a superordinate identity [or *new*

The Phileo, or "soul love," is divided into Perceptual
(mind) and Emotional (emotions) Oneness.

Figure 11.2

identity] is created. In a good marriage, each person contributes to the new entity (p. 52).

A good marriage brings about a "new entity," a "new marital identity," where each partner finds it difficult to think of himself or herself as separate from the other partner. That's exactly what God had planned when He created and defined the marriage bond: "For this cause a man shall leave his father and his mother, and shall cleave to his wife; and they shall become one flesh" (Genesis 2:24). This implies a process, as though God might go on to say, "And as you are fruitful and multiply, your offspring will learn, by way of your example, the art of oneness. Then, *they* will choose a partner. The man will leave his home and start all over again. The two shall become one, and *they* will be fruitful and multiply, passing on to *their* children the art of oneness." Leaving, cleaving, and receiving—a simple plan for success.

The female-man is different from the male-man in every area where we are to create this new entity, this oneness—except spiritually. In the physical area, the male is admonished to "honor" the female as the weaker sex (1 Peter 3:7). I'm built differently. My body has convex and concave surfaces unlike that of the male, and he is generally stronger than I am.

The casual observer would also consider me the weaker of the two sexes emotionally. This is not true. I am more emotionally oriented than a man (and that's *good)*, but despite being labeled "emotionally flighty," I often serve as the emotional *anchor* and many times will wind up pulling *him* through the traumatic experiences in life.

Finally, I am perceptually different from the male. I tend to have an intuitive nature that is beyond his comprehension. He can't believe I could arrive at a certain conclusion without going through ten logical steps! In fact, if he pressures me and says, "Explain your position. Give me the steps you took to get your answer," I'm often hard-pressed to satisfy his logical leanings! (An adjective that will generally surface in such an encounter is "stupid.") I am also typically a "people-centered" person and am more sensitive to the emotional needs of others than their logical needs (also beyond the male's comprehension).

Now you may be thinking, *That's not the way I am at all.* Well, let's *do* take into account the *flesh,* because we have all developed patterns in our tenure here on earth that can effectively bury the innate characteristics that were planted in each of us by God. He molded our perceptual and emotional differences just as surely as He molded our physical differences.

Becoming Spiritually One: Agape Love

Spiritually, the male's and female's needs are the same: to know God and to be secure in His love. Every facet of our lives will be determined by our spirit-life— that is, by our relationship to God and to His Son, Jesus. And our spiritual oneness makes oneness in the other areas compelling *and* attainable.

When my spirit is pervaded with the Spirit of Jesus and when my husband's spirit is pervaded with the Spirit of Jesus, we then become "one spirit with Him" (1 Corinthians 6:17). Our goals, our desires, and our attitudes will be the same, but because we are different in the other areas (physically, emotionally, and perceptually), there will always be two different approaches to those goals; there will be two different needs, two different emotions, two different perceptions. And yet understanding and mutual give-and-take will be possible because of our oneness of spirit.

> Have this attitude in yourselves, which was also in Christ Jesus, who, although He existed in the form of God, did not regard equality with God a thing to be grasped, but emptied Himself, taking the form of a bond-servant, and being made in the likeness of men. And being found in appearance as a man, He humbled Himself by becoming obedient to the point of death, even death on a cross (Philippians 2:5-8).

This spiritual "attitude" is the essence of spiritual oneness. It is *agape* love, unconditional love, and it is already ours because of our identity in Jesus: giving, self-denial, servitude, and humility all practiced willingly, motivated by love. And this love is *not* a feeling we must somehow "work up"; it's not the impossible dream, the unattainable ideal. *It is inside you.* Jesus is the only one who has lived or could *ever* live the Christian life.

Your instructions? Since He is now your life, you simply allow Him, by choosing to do so with your free will, to live that life and that love through you. You let it flow out, believing by faith that He will be your very life.

While practicing this attitude of being spiritually one, God promises to conform us to the image of His Son, Jesus. According to 2 Corinthians 3:18, we are being "transformed," changed step by step, glory by glory, into His image. If I am being changed into His likeness and my husband is being changed into His likeness, we will eventually both be like Him, and the *three of us* will be *one!* One + one + one = one.

In *The Changed Life*, author Henry Drummond says, "Every man's character remains as it is, or continues in the direction in which it is going, until it is compelled by *impressed forces* to change that state" (emphasis added). Since Bill and I are one, as he goes through this process of being conformed to the image of Jesus, I feel it; as I go through this process of change, he feels it. For example, being greedy may not be one of *my* flesh problems, but if my husband has this un-Christlike trait, I will probably have to endure the same painful "impressed forces" God allows to come into *his* life to alert him of his greed.

What might some of those forces be? Anything that would cause him to realize that material possessions aren't that important: the near loss of a child, a severe illness, or any crisis experience that brings him to the point of saying, "I realize, now, that 'things' are not where happiness lies." The impressed force brought about change, but my husband would not have been the only one involved in that learning experience—I would have been at the hospital, too. We learn *together*. We hurt *together*. We weep *together*. But then, we also rejoice *together!*

What Drummond calls "impressed forces" falls under the category of what the apostle Paul calls "all things" in the following passage from his letter to the Romans:

> And we know that God causes all things to work together for good to those who love God, to those who are called according to His purpose. For whom He foreknew, He also predestined to become conformed to the image of His Son, that He might be the first-born among many brethren (Romans 8:28,29).

It is likely that I will, at times, be that "impressed force" which causes my husband to fold, give in, cry out to God, and change; and he will, at times, be the impressed force in my life. This is part of God's plan for being spiritually one. When Bill and I began our epic journey over uncharted seas (when we got married), you'll remember that I had developed a pattern for being a supersensitive person (my unique version of the flesh), and Bill had developed a pattern for being a supercritical person (this was *his* flesh). I couldn't do anything to please him, and if I ever did come within reach of his standards, he raised them higher. My biscuits were *never* quite the right color, my green beans *never* had the right label, and my behavior was *always* a bit lacking in some area. But, of course, Bill couldn't say one word even hinting at criticism without adverse reactions from me (i.e., pouting, crying, packing, depression, or maybe spending a little money—the most effective retaliation).

My prayer life: "God, change Bill. I can't do a thing to please the man. He is destroying me."

Bill's prayer life: "God, change Anabel. I can't make any kind of helpful suggestion around here!"

Let me ask you something: Is being supersensitive a Christlike characteristic? No way! Well, then, is being supercritical a Christlike characteristic? Hardly. Now, in order for me to become aware of that sin of supersensitivity in my life, God had to allow a few "all things" to come into my life—or maybe an "impressed force." It just so happens that the force God chose to use was about five feet, 11 inches tall, weighed 185 pounds, and looked just like my husband. In order for Bill to become aware of his sin of being supercritical, God allowed an impressed force to come into his life. The force God chose to use was five feet, five-and-a-half inches, weighed around 124 pounds, and just happened to be me, his wife!

What if God had allowed me to marry a man who was so "considerate" of me that he *never* made even the slightest critical comment concerning anything I did or said? For example, suppose someone at church said something that hurt my feelings. My husband would quickly sympathize and suggest we change churches. Or if the woman whose desk was next to mine at work was critical and made life miserable for me, he would suggest I change jobs. A husband like that would have reinforced that wall around my un-Christlike supersensitivity, whisking me away from any confrontation I might encounter, screening me from these "cruel" people in my life. With such a husband, would I have ever realized that my supersensitive flesh was ungodly? No.

And if God had allowed Bill to marry a leather-skinned woman who, after his second cutting remark, would say, "Okay for you, Buster! Make your own biscuits," would he ever have cried out to God, having realized that his supercritical flesh was ungodly? No. He would have expanded his venomous vocabulary, and word battles would have raged around the happy home as he fiercely pursued his self-appointed task of humbling her, defeating her, destroying her—proving to himself his masculinity.

God was using Bill's critical tongue to remove an ugly, un-Christlike blemish on Anabel. Manly Beasley called this "heavenly sandpaper." Bill's critical tongue was the tool—the sandpaper, the impressed force, the "all things"—that God chose to use in my life in order to conform me to the image of His Son. In the same way, my supersensitivity was the sandpaper working on Bill's ugly blemish.

When Bill and I *finally* realized what God was up to in our lives, our prayers changed. Anabel: "God, please take away my hypersensitivity, that part of me that whimpers and whines and causes such unrest in our home." Bill: "Please deliver me from this critical tongue, Lord. I don't want to lash out at Anabel and hurt her; this is an abomination to me." And the impressed forces brought about the desire to change, as do all His ways when we are *open* to them.

Being spiritually one is the beginning of the story as God wrote it, and it ends—as we would like all our stories to end—"and they lived happily ever after." Your husband may choose not to be in the play. Never mind, you're still the Sleeping Beauty. Play your part well. You don't write the endings.

Becoming Physically One: Eros Love

While God conforms us to the image of His Son, there is also a physical oneness to be developed—a unity that will complete and magnify the other areas of our oneness.

> Do you not know that your bodies are members of Christ? Shall I then take away the members of Christ and make them members of a harlot? May it never be! Or do you not know that the one who joins himself to a harlot is one body with her? For He says, "The two will become one flesh" (1 Corinthians 6:15,16).

There can be no mistaking that Paul is talking about sexual purity and physical oneness through sexual intercourse in these verses. For some of us, discussing such private things can be uncomfortable. Why? Because we have allowed the world to press us into its mold and have come to think of this act of love from the world's viewpoint instead of from God's viewpoint. C.S. Lewis wrote,

The monstrosity of sexual intercourse outside of marriage is that those who indulge in it
are trying to isolate one kind of union (the sexual) from all the other kinds of union which
were intended to go along with it and make up
the total union. The Christian attitude does not
mean that there is anything wrong about sexual
pleasure, any more than about the pleasure of
eating. It means that you must not isolate that
pleasure and try to get it by itself, any more
than you ought to try to get the pleasure of
taste without swallowing and digesting, by
chewing things and spitting them out again.[2]

As Lewis said, the world typically would have us
"isolate" the sex act, separating it from the other areas of
oneness. But God intends for sexual intercourse to be the
ultimate in the giving of yourself to your husband: It is
that level of giving which serves to seal your vow, to bond
you together and allow you to express your love in its
entirety. It is a beautiful expression of love between husband and wife. It is behavior acceptable before God, insti-
tuted by God, observed by God, and pleasing to God.
There should be no shame involved. It should certainly be a
personal and intimate part of your life, but not because
it's "dirty" or "something that you just shouldn't talk
about."

It is doubtful that there is one woman reading this
book who does not have negative patterns about sex
burned into her memory banks. Perhaps your Victorian
mother, who avoided any reference to sex like a dreaded
plague, had a profound influence on what you think
about sex. As a result, you may have a voracious sex drive,
or you may be totally uninterested, reluctant, and frigid.

Perhaps you were sexually abused or "misused" as you were growing up, and sex for you now is one terrible memory.

There are any number of negative patterns that can develop concerning sex, patterns that can potentially control your relationship with your husband and damage the extraordinary beauty of your physical oneness. These destructive patterns often run deep, but, my dear one, they are patterns. *They are not you.* You are not to allow them to control you any more than I am to allow my patterns of supersensitivity to control me. Do you remember your true identity? Do you remember how Satan "speaks" to you? Do you remember that these patterns are not you? That they are your flesh? (If you have trouble remembering the answers to these questions, go back and review Chapters 4 and 5.)

God's plan for sexual compatibility is responding to each other's needs. Women view sex so differently than men do. For a woman, sex begins early in the morning when her husband is gentle and appreciative; it builds through the day when he listens to her, when he meets her for lunch, when he talks to her, when he shows interest in her plans, ideas, and concerns. Tenderness, thoughtfulness, and meaningful interaction culminate in her longing to give herself to him, to express her love for him sexually. But husbands may often be ignorant of or insensitive to these needs of their wives—the very needs that stimulate the desire for intimacy and physical oneness. They attempt to control their wives through guilt or forced passion, getting their need met *their* way.

Women, on the other hand, will often use sex as a system of reward or punishment, controlling it their way. "If you've been nice to me, Husband, I will reward you with lovemaking. If you have not been nice to me, I will develop a headache." This is wrong. Your husband may desire sex because he saw a voluptuous female walking down the street or because his secretary was seductively dressed. And there is nothing degrading about this. God created the male to be sexually aroused by a visual stimulus, but this doesn't mean that he gloats lustfully, drools longingly, and fantasizes wildly over what he sees. It means, simply, that he has a physical need. What happens to you when you see a chocolate cake? Granted, there is a balance in responding to both the cake and the secretary (you don't eat half the platter, right? and your husband doesn't flirt with his secretary), but don't make something obscene of his desire or put him in a class with the sexually obsessed because he is stimulated by her appearance. Call him normal.

Furthermore, did you know that your husband may desperately need sex because a project he has been working on for the last six weeks failed? Or because his boss chewed him out at work? Or because he had to confront one of his employees? Sex is God-given therapy in every realm of oneness—spiritually, physically, emotionally, and perceptually. And it is one of the most effective ways you can minister to your husband, edifying him, encouraging him, assuring him that he is very much a man, that he is desirable and is still everything to you.

Sexual compatibility greatly influences the atmosphere of your relationship: Your husband's male ego will be content, his love for you will be enhanced, his sexual desires will be satisfied, and the tension will be significantly reduced for both parties. If your sexual relationship isn't all that you would like for it to be, then you should educate yourself in that area.

Let's say apple pie is your husband's favorite dessert

(he told you that many times during your courtship). Well, you've tried Aunt Betty's recipe, Grandma's recipe, a *Better Homes and Gardens* recipe, and numerous others. At last, you find *the* recipe and hear those infamous words, "Ah, just like Mama used to make." (Rather nauseating, isn't it?) In any case, you throw away all the other recipes because you have found what you and he together have been searching for. Preparing bedroom delicacies should be approached in much the same way. Try different ingredients, add your own touches, follow your creative impulses, read some good books (*Love Life* by Dr. Ed Wheat is excellent).

Physical oneness is the easiest oneness to achieve. There are millions of couples who are one only on the physical level, knowing nothing of the oneness that is possible through Jesus. The sexual act can be very superficial, very shallow, meeting a temporary need for a brief span of time; and tragically, many marriages don't survive when this area of oneness is violated. A man and woman can be physically one and yet never be vulnerable or open in those deeper areas of oneness—perceptually and emotionally. True physical oneness can only be experienced in all its beauty when those who join themselves together, becoming one flesh, know each other deeply and intimately in the other realms of oneness.

Becoming Perceptually One: Phileo Love

Be humble and gentle. Be patient with each other, making allowance for each other's faults because of your love. Try always to be led along together by the Holy Spirit, and so be at peace with one another. We are all parts of one body, we have the same Spirit, and we have all been called to the same glorious future (Ephesians 4:2-4, TLB).

Intercourse is not confined to a sexual experience. *Intercourse* means communication, and some neat things happen when we are *perceptually* one, when our communication is grounded in a conscious awareness of the other person's needs and ways: Our identity flourishes, and we believe we are important to someone; our sense of security and our need for belonging are fulfilled; respect, appreciation, and understanding become a part of our relationship; and we find ourselves content just to be together, accepted. We can ride in the car and not feel compelled to make conversation; we are comfortable with each other's silence. He knows I'm proud of him, and I know he's not going to lash out at me.

There sometimes seems to be a perceptual unity before marriage that fades when the door to the honeymoon cottage closes:

> Before we were married, Husband, when we went fishing you put the worm on my hook for me, sitting close, sometimes with your arms around me. When we went to the ball game, there wasn't any of this sitting with your buddies while all of us girls huddled together and talked about recipes. No, before we were married, Husband, you were patient with me when I asked questions: "Who are the men in the striped shirts?" You seemed to delight in eating popcorn out of the same sack.
>
> What happened? You never ask me to go fishing with you anymore; but then, that's all right, because I don't want to go with you if

everything I do is wrong or stupid. (I remember the time I was put in the bow of the boat with explicit instructions on just how to carry out a certain assignment—a job more along the lines of "mission impossible" for a novice who didn't know the bow from the stern. We wound up in the fork of a tree with the boat and all the fishing gear on the bottom of the river. Sigh.)

I'd rather not go if I'm expected to cook for your 14 deer-hunting friends, or if my only job assignment is to watch you ski and tell you how good you are. Let me stay home. I'd rather walk the dog around the block, thank you.

Being perceptually one means knowing your spouse's needs and respecting them. It means being considerate and thoughtful and kind. It means working at being together.

This oneness is a deeper, more difficult union than being physically one: I can share with you and you won't laugh at me; I can tell you about my hurts and you'll listen; I can dream my dreams and you'll want to be part of them. It entails vulnerability, the baring of your soul. It concerns absolute transparency, unabashed communication, complete understanding. Being perceptually one means sharing freely without fear. It means enjoying being together. It means, "Not only do I love you, I like you. You are my dearest friend."

Jesus spoke of how He and His Father were one: "That they may be one, just as We are one" (see John 17:21); and again He said, "I and the Father are one" (John 10:30). Individuals, separate—the Father and Son—and yet one. How was this so? In part, it was that they had one purpose, one hope, one goal, and this is being perceptually one. The Father and the Son had a certain implicit *singleness of will* or *common mind-set,* as though they sat down and planned everything out prior to the event, understanding each other completely, intuitively. And then they committed themselves to carrying it out—*together.* "I do not seek My own will, but the will of Him who sent Me" (John 5:30). A singleness of will.

There are a lot of marriages where there is a singleness of will, where the goals, purposes, and dreams are the same: "We, John and Mary, as man and wife, do hereby commit ourselves to these common goals, to this singleness of will: The ladder of success is open to us, and we will, no matter what the cost, climb it rung by rung! Our children will be given every chance to excel in their chosen field, from baseball camp to music seminars. They shall have the finest educational opportunities, the most prominent facilities available. A split-level home with three garages and a large car for every garage is our ultimate desire." That's being perceptually one, isn't it? It's a oneness that isn't under the umbrella of the spiritual realm, but it is a form of oneness.

When Bill became a Christian, we started our lives all over again, renewing our vows to each other and to God. We became perceptually one. We had a common goal, a singleness of will: for our marriage, that it would glorify God; for our lives as individuals, that we would be vessels for His use; and for our children, that they might come to know God and His Son, Jesus, as reality in their lives. All our energies would bend to these goals. Our family was to be Christ-centered—a singleness of will.

Effort. Patience. Understanding. Listening. Transparency. Vulnerability. A singleness of will. These are the pieces that, put together, make perceptual oneness. Again, your husband may not share even the slightest interest with you as you think about being one, and this makes the process more difficult and seem all the more hopeless. Only Christ, living through you, can play your part. And Christ living through you *will*—He's waiting for you to let Him do it all for you.

Becoming One Emotionally: Phileo Love

Your body is acutely aware of everything that happens to it: When your stomach hurts, your whole body knows it, and immediate steps are taken by all concerned to alleviate the pain. You are a single unit, undivided, and you are sensitive to every touch of the skin. You are *one*. Paul, being the marvelous teacher that he was, knew we would be able to understand this analogy, so he used it to explain to the Ephesians what it means to be one with your spouse:

> That is how husbands should treat their wives, loving them as parts of themselves. For since a man and his wife are now one, a man is really doing himself a favor and loving himself when he loves his wife. No one hates his own body but lovingly cares for it, just as Christ cares for his body the church, of which we are parts (Ephesians 5:28-30, TLB).

"Does my husband know how badly I'm hurting? Does he care?"

"Does my wife realize how she is destroying me? Does she care?"

A new dimension is not miraculously added to the young husband's thinking process at the wedding ceremony. He doesn't suddenly become aware that his sphere of sensitivity includes the woman he has just taken as his wife. Being emotionally one is a still higher oneness than that of being physically or perceptually one, and for the male, this sensitivity is generally a learning process which calls for desire, communication, practice, humility, and prayer.

I didn't know this when I got married, and for many years my heart-cry was the same as I'm sure yours has been: *You just don't understand me!* I would give, give, and give again, but when a need surfaced in *my* life, he didn't even seem to be *aware* of it! And then he would say, "But Honey, I can't *know* what you're feeling."

How I longed to talk with him, to work out our differences, to share my pain with him and become sensitive to *his* pain. Invariably, the conversation would end with my crying and blurting out, "Why I ever share anything with you and expect you to be understanding is beyond me! Never, never, never again!" (I was serious. I meant it!) But "again" would eventually come around, and once more he would wind up proclaiming his innocence.

He was right, you know. The male isn't adequately equipped when it comes to sensing, to being sensitive to, the emotional needs of the female. (There may be exceptions to the rule—and what a nice exception for the lucky woman!) Most women can tell when their husband walks through the door how his day has been and what his emotional state is like. But the wife may have to be lying on the bed, washcloth over her eyes, perhaps even emitting a low moan, before he will take note and say, "Have a hard day, Honey?" (That's a slight overstatement, but you get the picture.)

A mother can train her sons to be emotionally sensitive to the female, and congratulations if you marry one who has already been taught the art. Generally, the hours are long and the arguments heated because of this emotional breakdown in communication, because of this lack of emotional oneness.

>**She:** "Why did you do that tonight?"
>**He:** "What did I do?"
>**She:** "Oh, come on, you're smarter than that!"
>**He:** "What are you talking about? What did I do to upset you?"
>**She:** "Surely you can't be serious! How can you hurt me like that and not even know it?"

Bill and I were so different when we got married. He was comfortable in any social setting; I always felt like a teenager on her first date. If he had only stayed with me, I would not have minded going to all the social functions he delighted in attending. I needed his security. He did this during our dating days; I was his badge of honor. But things changed after the conquest was over.

"Wow! Great fun!" Bill would say. "Did you have a good time, Honey?"

"Well, not really." (He hadn't noticed that I was alone most of the evening or in the kitchen or in the rest room ten times.)

"Why not?"

"I'm so uncomfortable in situations like that. If you'd just let me hang onto your arm—be with you—I'd enjoy myself a lot more." He couldn't understand me and didn't want to try at that point in our marriage. He was insensitive to my need. We were not emotionally one.

How different it is now. It's as though sometimes the shoe is on the other foot. Bill is acutely aware of this emotional need, so much so that I rarely ever feel uncomfortable anymore. I am confident of his love, his concern, and his desire to minister to me, and this gives *me* confidence in social gatherings. All I need to do is casually walk over to him, slip my arm into his, and he knows that I want to be near him, to be secure in his presence. This oneness wasn't achieved without heartache and compassion, without understanding our emotional needs and allowing Christ to meet those needs through us.

First, the *desire* to achieve this oneness must be present: "Honey, I'd like to work at becoming one in this area. How about you?" Then, we must *communicate*. It's a "feelings" awareness; I must tell him how I feel, and then listen as he tells me how he feels (and the process may begin with me doing all the listening). This can be stressful: "Honey, it really bothers me when you finish my sentences for me. People wonder if I'm stupid or something when you dominate the conversation like you do. A man likes to feel as though he's able to talk for himself, you know?" (That hurts!)

After receiving what he says (and not leaping to my own defense), I must *practice*. This means that I must watch myself when I'm in a group and try not to talk so much, especially when someone asks my husband a direct question. So what if he doesn't get all the facts right! He told me it hurts him, and I don't want to hurt him. But invariably I'll blow it (or he'll blow it in some area where I've asked him to be careful): "I'm so sorry, Honey. I don't want to do that. I realize it must be very embarrassing to you. Forgive me?" Apologies must readily be accepted, not insisting that any hurt was intentional: "That's all right, Babe. You did a lot better tonight. We should have tried this years ago. We'll make it." Believe me, this requires *humility* on the part of both parties—and *prayer*: "Lord, please help me. I don't want to hurt my husband this way. Work on this problem through me."

As a wife, I must be just as sensitive to my husband's needs as I long for him to be to mine, and because of my "intuitive nature" and sensitivity to the "heart" needs of others, I am more equipped for emotional oneness than he is. This is my strength and my husband's weakness. My practice will be his training.

Your Commitment to Oneness

I can't fully comprehend it, but God said we are one, and *that makes it so.* My responsibility? To seek God's diagnosis for my starving dreams, for the deep longings of my heart, for my crippled marriage. My heavenly Father knows that I hurt—and He cares. I must cast all these burdens onto Him, and then I must trust *Him* to renew or restore, to bring beauty from ashes, to transform, to fashion my marriage after *His* pattern—or to give me the wisdom, the strength, the grace, the desire, and the tenacity to live with my "unloving" husband.

A schismatic body—divided, torn, separated—cannot function according to God's directive; it cannot expect to know the thrill of marriage, the fulfillment, the beauty of this intricate creation operating at maximum capacity. Marriage is not that romantic "50-50" deal; it isn't even that "giving yourself 100 percent" plan. God says, "Where once there were two, now there is one."

Spiritually: "Lord, I pray that You will so fill me with Your breath, Your mind, Your Spirit, that I will think only Your thoughts and live Your life, finding therein my own life, infinitely glorified. With Your life indwelling me, I ask that the fragrance of Your love permeate every facet of my life, bringing about the beauty of our oneness."

Physically: "Lord, minister to my husband through

me. Let me meet his needs by giving of myself for *his* fulfillment! Don't ever let him feel compelled to meet this need for physical intimacy elsewhere."

Perceptually: "Father, cause me to become more and more determined to know You, to become more deeply and intimately acquainted with You, perceiving, recognizing, and understanding the wonders of Your Person more strongly and more clearly. For as I walk in the closeness of Your presence, You will remind me of my commitment to my husband, to knowing him and knowing his needs."

Emotionally: "Lord, give me discernment, understanding, wisdom, tenderness, and gentleness that I may be constantly and keenly aware of my husband's deepest desires and hurts."

Lord, make me an instrument of Your peace. Where there is hatred, let me sow love; where there is injury, pardon; where there is doubt, faith; where there is despair, hope; where there is darkness, light; and where there is sadness, joy.

Grant that I may not so much seek to be consoled as to console; to be understood as to understand; to be loved as to love. For it is in giving that we receive, it is in pardoning that we are pardoned, and it is in dying that we are raised to eternal life.

—St. Francis of Assisi

12

Three Needs

A man takes a wife thinking the woman he has chosen will never change; a woman takes a husband thinking the man she has chosen can be changed.

Unshakable
+ Unconditional
+ Unfathomable
+ Unsinkable
+ Unbelievable
+ Unending
+ Unsurpassed
+ Unlimited
+ Unchangeable
= Agape Love

An impressive list, isn't it? But the most incredible thing about this equation is that it is all *yours* because of Christ, the personification of that amazing *agape* love who lives inside you! As you choose to walk in this *agape* love (trusting and allowing the God-man, Jesus, to control you, to live that love through you), certain characteristics will become evident: You'll find yourself wanting to give rather than receive; you'll want to serve others rather than think only of yourself; you'll want others to feel important rather than calling attention to yourself or considering yourself as deserving or special; and you'll be *willing* to do all this simply because of your *agape* love. In other words, you won't be pursuing *your* needs, thinking about *your* rights, or always evaluating *his* responsibilities. Your goal will be focused, single: that Jesus Christ might express love for your husband through you.

We've talked about what it means to become one spiritually, one physically, one perceptually, and one emotionally. Now, how do we go about accomplishing this oneness in our marriage? How can we be a positive influence in the process? What are some practical things we can do to bring it about?

We must search out the part we are to play, our role. God called both the man and woman "Man," establishing their equality; then, He established different roles for them. We have a script to follow just as surely as Julie Andrews did in *The Sound of Music*, and what a mess the movie would have been if she had insisted on playing Captain von Trapp's role.

Before you read any further, remember that your power to play your part will be the result of your being one spiritually with Christ: "The one who joins himself to the Lord is one spirit with Him" (1 Corinthians 6:17). This is the oneness that is absolutely *required* for success in other areas of oneness. "But, Anabel, my husband is not a Christian," or, "My husband isn't 'walking with the Lord.' He's not interested in these things."

What do you do?

First of all, you are under submission to God, and that means you are to be obedient in spite of your husband's spiritual condition. Obedience to God is not conditional. "But, Anabel . . ." No. By placing yourself under God's authority, you will enable Him to work through you to touch your husband's life. Above all, remember that you aren't in this by yourself. He's going to do it all for you, right?

Creating Oneness

Human beings have three basic needs: the need to *belong* (or be loved), the need for a sense of *competency*, and the need to know their lives have *value*. These needs were programmed into us by God, and they complement the very areas of oneness we've been discussing. Your role—assigned to you by God and energized by the indwelling Christ—is to meet these needs in your husband's life. As you allow Christ to live through you, trusting *Him* to minister to your husband, to love him and fulfill these needs, you will communicate to your husband that you enjoy him, respect him, and need him. Oneness will be birthed and nourished. (Birth only comes through travail—nourishment through constant, loving care. This process is not an easy one, but it is, oh, so satisfying.)

Belonging (physical oneness)
She: "I'm glad you're my husband."
He: *She enjoys me; she likes being with me.*

Competency (perceptual oneness)
She: "Your wisdom in such matters is incredible."
He: *She respects me.*

Value (emotional oneness)
   She: "I am so proud of you."
   He: *She needs me.*

I Need to Belong
("I'm glad you're my husband.")

She Loves Me

Belonging and *acceptance* are synonymous in a way: "When you *accept* me, I *belong* to you, your group; I'm in your sphere of friends; I'm not by myself—somebody *loves* me. And not only do I belong to someone, but someone belongs to me as well." This need can be met in many ways and on many levels—social groups, clubs, the church, special friends. But I'm supposed to be the one who meets this need most effectively in my husband's life.

I doubt many of you remember the song "Bill" from the Broadway play *Showboat* (naturally, it's one of our songs):

> But along came Bill, he's not the type at all.
> You'd meet him on the street and never notice him.
> His form and face, his manly grace,
> Are not the kind that you would find in a statue.
> And I can't explain,
> It's surely not his brain
> That makes me thrill.
> I love him because he's wonderful,
> Because he's just my Bill.[1]

If you truly *love* someone, you don't require him to perform a certain way to merit your acceptance; you don't demand that he meet your standards for physical appearance; you don't love him because of his achievements.

Granted, these things may *attract* you to him, but if you base your great expectations for marriage and love on one of these attractions, you will probably be very disillusioned. You draw him into your circle of love, making him part of your world, just because of who he is.

> If thou must love me, let it be for nought
> Except for love's sake only.
> —Elizabeth Barrett Browning

She Loves Me Not

Not to accept your husband is to reject him. It's just that simple. He will sense your rejection through perceived attitudes (what he *thinks* you're thinking, whether you're thinking that or not), your overt actions, and your covert actions. And the little "underhanded" things you may do, the covert actions, scream just as loudly and have the same effect as overt rejection: cruel, crippling, destructive. He will know if you are simply "putting up with him"; he will know if you are passively enduring his company—none of this I'm-so-glad-you're-my-husband bit. You may not tell him this is the way you feel, but communication is not limited to words. You tell him this in subtle ways:

- Act bored, disinterested.
- Be noncommunicative. But let others enter the scene and suddenly you're a different person: laughing, talking, demonstrative, interesting, excited about the evening.
- Don't do things with him: "Oh, he has his interests, and I have mine." Stay back in the bedroom, working, instead of setting up shop in the den with him while he watches the ball game:

"It's just so much trouble to move all of my para-phernalia to the den for just one night!"

- Go back to school evenings.
- Get a part-time job that demands every free min-ute.
- Go to the spa four evenings a week.
- Don't talk with him; talk on the phone all evening.
- Make it your habit to go to bed early and read. Whether it's a book, a magazine, or a Bible, the results will be the same.

He'll get the message: *She doesn't like to be with me. I don't belong here. She doesn't love me.*

It's Never Too Late to Rehabilitate

Do you want to change? Your emotions may be say-ing, "Nope! I don't enjoy his company, and I don't feel like doing anything with him!" *But we're going on faith and commitment, not feeling.* What's your mission? *Agape* love. Does Christ desire this change? Yes. Can Christ, liv-ing through you, accomplish it? Yes. Will He bring it about? Yes, if you'll trust Him, if you'll ask Him.

Let your husband know that you enjoy his company, that he *belongs* to you:

- Plan times when just the two of you can be together.
- Ask to be with him, to go to the store or run an errand with him just so you can enjoy his com-pany: "If you'll wait five minutes, I'll go with you!"
- Talk him into a weekend getaway—just the two of you—and buy some pretty, filmy lingerie for a nice surprise.

- Tell him, "I like it when you go shopping with me. It's fun to drive around and be together, isn't it?"
- Go for yogurt, a picnic in the park, a scenic drive, a boat ride, "people watching" at the mall, a walk around the block, fishing, boating, hunting, biking, a baseball game, a football game, a basketball game, a golf match, stock car racing, a rodeo, a car museum, a train museum, a plane museum, an antique mall, a planetarium, a science-fiction movie, working in the garage, walking the dogs . . .

So very simple. But by doing these things, by making this effort, what will you be saying to your husband? *I like being with you.* Communication on this level takes *work*, but remember that it is Christ in and through you which makes it possible, attainable.

There are many areas where you can meet your husband's need to belong, but perhaps the most important is being physically attractive and physically affectionate. It's so easy to become careless about how we look: "Well, he doesn't knock himself out trying to keep trim and slim. If he can go around sloppy, why can't I?" Reason #1: When you're pleased with your physical appearance, your entire outlook on life changes. Reason #2: Men are physically attracted to physically attractive women.

Your script calls for you to be pleasing to your husband in the way you look. "But he doesn't care, Anabel. I could look like Scarlet O'Hara, and he wouldn't bat an eye." I'm sure some of you have husbands who are thoughtless, unkind, and uncommunicative—in short, general clods. I'm sorry. But you can begin the process of change by asking, "What would you like me to wear,

Honey?" "What do you think of my hair this way?" "Do these shoes look all right with this dress?" You will be letting him know that you care about how you look, that you want to be physically attractive to him.

Don't misjudge your husband's need for you to be physically attractive to him. (You want your husband to look nice for you, right?) God designed the male to respond to the visual stimulus of the female. Sensuous movements and seductive dress—even a hug at church—can excite his sexual impulses. Holding a man's arm may offer security to a woman, but it may be physically stimulating to a man. This is the way he was designed. This is said in his defense.

Making yourself physically attractive for your husband and being physically affectionate toward him isn't always that easy. It takes initiative. It takes determination. For starters in the affectionate area, try holding his hand at the movies or in church. Give him a "welcome home kiss," or sit close to him on the divan instead of sitting in your favorite chair. "It's *his* chair that's the problem, Anabel! It's too small for two, and you couldn't budge him out of it if you had to!" Okay. Plop down in his lap or invite him to sit with you.

There are three cardinal rules to remember in the physical area: (1) be available, (2) be agreeable, and (3) be sexually aggressive (occasionally). This calls for creativity. Get in the shower with him—that should startle him just a tad!

And with the passing years: "You're growing old, Husband. Your face is getting crinkled, your chin is sagging, and your waistline seems to be sagging, too. I want you to know something. None of that matters to me. I love you—just the way you are."

And with unforeseen circumstances: "You may be in a car wreck, burned and physically incapacitated; you may have a stroke and not be able to talk to me anymore; you may come home from work without a job. I want you to know something. This doesn't change my love for you. You're my husband 'for richer or poorer, in sickness and in health.' I meant those words when I said, 'I do.' I'm committed to you. I love you. You *belong* to me."

I Need to Feel Competent
("Your wisdom in such matters is incredible!")

She Respects Me

The male was programmed by God for leadership (if you doubt this, go observe a first-grade class at recess). It is his *need,* not his right. If you, as his wife, choose not to meet this need (or to usurp his role), then mark my words: Your husband will get it met elsewhere.

Now, you may be thinking, *How utterly archaic! This is the twentieth century, not the Dark Ages! Woman has come a long way since your day, Anabel.* You're right; it is archaic. In fact, I'm going back to the first century for my material, checking with the One who made the machine. He designed it. He knows how it works most effectively. Archaic or not, the failure of one out of every two marriages proves that our twentieth-century program isn't working too well. We're doing something wrong. We're making some big mistakes, and one of them is usurping the husband's role as leader.

A wife can either encourage her husband to assume this God-given role of leadership, or she can compete with him for it. Unfortunately, this "competition" is prevalent and makes for one of today's most maligned areas in the male/female relationship. For the little boy whose mother "wears the pants" in the family, the effects begin before he can say, "Mama," and the flesh patterns he may develop can be tragic:

1. He may choose the route of homosexuality because he sees himself as totally incapable of ever performing as a male, of ever becoming stronger than his competitive, aggressive, dominant mother (who represents all females to him).

2. He may choose to become a passive male, doubting his ability to perform in the male role and too threatened to exert authority or to take a position of leadership.

3. He may develop strong "macho" tendencies and be hostile toward females, especially strong females who compete for his role. (Do you remember Bill's old habit patterns?) For understanding these patterns and how to deal with them, I would highly recommend *Lifetime Guarantee* by Bill (my handsome husband) Gillham (Harvest House, 1993).

You didn't enter the marriage relationship determined to break your husband's spirit or destroy him (just a few minor changes here and there, right?). But if, instead of creating an atmosphere for leadership, you undermine this need of your husband, he will perceive you as emasculating him. He will believe that you consider him incompetent. And he will think this, regardless of whether it is deliberate on your part or not. Your competency in carrying out *his* role, your casual remarks about *his* ineptness, or direct attacks on *his* ability will not embarrass him into changing—it will only embarrass him. It will only eat away at his sense of competency.

- Everyone's in the kitchen, including George: "Oh, your kitchen drawers pull out so smoothly. George has been promising to fix mine for the last eight months! I wonder if your husband would hire out for the day" (forced laughter).
- A small party, and her husband can hear her talking several feet away: "Men seem to think they're gifted in every area. Well, I have one who certainly isn't."
- She's chatting on the phone in the other room, but her husband can hear her every word: "If I can keep my husband from playing the handyman role, the home runs a lot smoother. You talk about being all thumbs!"

You can constantly communicate, in so many sly ways, that *your* plan, *your* way, is better than his—even the route to the grocery store. And you can always dredge up his major "flop" (when "once upon a time" he *did* undertake a project), refusing to let him forget his failure. I was an expert at "second guessing" (that's what we call it around our house, and I'm certainly not immune to such behavior now). Bill would make a decision, and I would have a better one.

That's the recipe for major destruction, but you don't have to keep dishing it out. How about some plans to alter the menu? (Remember, *you* can't, but Christ can!)

- Ask his advice and say something like, "Well, that isn't the plan I had, but yours seems better. Yes. I'd rather do it your way."
- Be careful around your friends, especially your close friends, not to make critical "husband" remarks or discuss his poor performance.

- Watch your luncheon menu with the girls. Never order "chopped husband."
- When you're out for the evening, whether alone or with a group, don't "snip" at him constantly. Do you know what will happen? He'll start "snipping" back.
- In a shaky, let's-do-it-together redecorating project, try saying, "That's looking so nice! We're learning to wallpaper slowly but surely, aren't we, Sugar? You'll never know how much I appreciate your help."
- When he suggests going out for supper to the Italian buffet, say, "That sounds good," instead of, "I don't want pasta." That wasn't your approach during the "dating days," was it? You want him to be "like he was before he got you into the castle with the drawbridge up"? Perhaps he would like that, too.

Defuse or Detonate

I think of the time I was fixing supper and had everything under control, so I decided to step out front and to see how Bill was getting along in the "bicycle repair business." When I stepped out the door, he looked up and said, "Boy, am I glad to see you. I need some help." (Now, through the years I had learned one thing very well: I do not "help" the way Bill likes someone to help.) My emotions start their ascent, and I wish I had stayed inside.

He's all crouched down in an awkward position and says to me, "I need you to shim this screw here."

Shem? Well, there's Shem, Ham, and Japheth—that's the only "shem" in my vocabulary.

"I don't see what you mean, Honey."

He can move only his little finger, so pointing as best he can, he says, once again, "This screw. I need you to shim it for me."

"I'm sorry. I don't understand." My emotions are doing quite well on their upward climb—probably three-quarters of the way to the top. He finally gets me to understand (increased decibels and terse statements, guaranteed to prod the emotions, included). Now I'm on the pavement, holding the screwdriver, and he's in the garage getting whatever mysterious thing it is he needs to complete his work.

What's going on inside me? Bad things. I want to let him know he has hurt me, and several *destructive* ways to do that are *given* to me (remember where they come from?), like, "I just never do things to please you, do I, Bill?" (I've chosen that one many times before, and I know the results: another ruined, tension-filled evening in the Gillham household.) Allowing Christ to be my life (and I do so want Him to control me), another alternative comes to mind—a balm, a positive statement, muttered through gritted teeth, maybe, with emotions stomping their feet, demanding that I retaliate. "It amazes me, the way you can fix these broken bikes, Hon." (I decide to use the balm instead of the bomb. It wasn't easy!)

You talk about defusing a tense situation! Even now, in retelling the story, I get a surge of relief. Those few words set me free. (Of course, Bill was oblivious to the proceedings that were going on inside me where the emotions were making their way to the top.) That statement was not easy to make, and there is no way I could have made it outside of the power that is mine because of Christ.

Letting Him do it for you works such miracles. Opting for the first "vengeance is mine" choice equals one time plus another time equals two times, plus several more times equals many times, plus many more times equals hundreds of such "little" episodes, which equals untotaled hours of tension, which equals divorce. *They build.* You store them up and then regurgitate them, and as you dwell on them, your emotions climb higher and higher. (Review time: Do you remember who makes sure you have all those incidents filed and ready for instant regurgitation? Who gives you those thoughts? Who delights in having a ringside seat, watching as you carry out his insidious plan? The Deceiver.)

The bicycle story had a happy ending for both of us: I didn't get depressed out of my tree, and Bill had a renewed sense of competency—his ability to repair a broken bicycle. We're talking about perception, and your husband needs to perceive that he is competent. But there's something you should know: The male and the female arrive at their perceptions from entirely different routes.

Generally speaking, a woman thinks with her heart. (Don't turn me off if you disagree—keep reading.) She is people-centered, and her "weakness" (I use this term loosely) is in her logic. The male complements this weakness as he deals more from logic than from the heart. He is generally intellectually centered, and his weakness is in his heart. Woman complements this weakness with her intuitive nature. For example, a situation arises that demands a calculated decision:

> **He:** "We've got to take care of this problem. I believe we should do this (step one), this (step two), and this (step three)."

She: "Well, I don't *feel* like that's what we should do."

He: "What do you mean you don't *feel* like we should do it this way?"

She: "I don't *feel right* about it, that's all."

He: "If you can't give me one reason, other than 'that's just the way I feel,' for why you think we should hold off on this, then forget it. We'll do it my way." (Definitely *his* way because Christ living through him would not be so short or show such lack of understanding. Wrong method.)

This man is failing to see that he and his wife are evaluating the problem from different perspectives: he from his logic, she from her intuitive insight. Both are God-given strengths designed to complement and complete the other, establishing a oneness. In no way is one superior to the other. Intuitive discernment is a beautiful and rare gift from God to us as women. If a man insists on making a decision without consulting his wife, he is making a decision without a full understanding of the problem! As someone once said, "That would be like calling the election before all the precincts were in." If you do not express yourself—what you see, how you see it, how you perceive the issue—you are withholding valuable input from the decision-making process.

Discussion is the key, with each one understanding the other's different approach. Who, then, after discussion time, makes the final decision? The husband, of course. "Why did you say 'of course' so quickly, Anabel?" This is his role; it's written into his script. God has given him the awesome responsibility of caring for his family, of providing for them, of protecting them.

How frustrating it would be not to have the authority to fulfill that responsibility. How defeating it would be to *know* you were supposed to be in charge, and yet to have no one pay any attention to you, to have no one recognize you as the authority figure—intimidated, cowed, robbed of that masculine trait by the very one God designed to edify, respect, and esteem you. As a wife, you must realize how completely out of God's plan you are if you are operating as the authority figure in your home. This is not your role.

"But Anabel, my husband is totally incapable of making decisions!" His mother probably thought so, too, and never gave him the opportunity to try, to fail, and to learn from his failure. Why don't you let him? Ask God to keep you from expressing your opinion, from interrupting his conversations, from talking too much, from insisting that you know what's best. Begin by using phrases like, "Tell me what you think"; "I'll have to ask my husband about it"; or the ultimate, "I'll let you answer that question, Honey. You could do it much better than I could."

How emasculating it must be for the man who never gets a chance to make a decision, or even to answer a question. You direct your eye contact to *him* and ask *him*, knowing he is capable of answering, but *she* says, in one way or another, "I'll handle this, Dear." Pity that man. There is nothing so sad as a man who has been stripped of his sense of competency.

There are only two alternatives: (1) You will allow your husband to be the authority figure; or (2) you will be the authority figure. The first is done out of willful obedience; the second is done out of willful *dis*obedience.

You are not to expect, demand, or desire a role of

leadership in your marriage. Because of Christ *in* you, you are a servant. Your position is one of service to God and your desire is to obey Him. This does not concern feelings, justice, or needs; it concerns obedience.

I Need to Feel Valued
("I am so proud of you.")

She Needs Me

> Praise: to commend the worth of; to extol in words.

> Praise: essential for the male; an innate need.

> Praise: possible through Christ; supernatural.

Someone has equated the emotions a woman experiences when her husband has an affair to the same emotions a man experiences when his wife refuses to praise him. You're probably saying, "No way do those compare, Anabel." Yes, they do. You see, when a man seeks out another female for sexual gratification, what he is often saying to his wife is this: "Your femininity is not satisfying to me; I'm going to find someone whose femininity *is* satisfying to me." The woman who refuses to praise her husband is saying the same thing: "Sorry. Your masculinity is not pleasing to me. I see nothing in you worth praising."

Let me share a letter with you:

Dear Anabel,

> I sat through your seminar listening as though you were speaking directly to me when you spoke of the "strong woman." Yes, I am a strong woman. I was raised by my divorced mother who was the epitome of independence

and strength. Need a man? Ha! That was not part of the program.

So I am an independent, strong-willed performer, even though I don't look it (I'm 5'2", 105 pounds). But I have a will of iron. There is a constant power struggle between my husband and me.

God spoke to me last night when you said someone compared the emotions a woman has when her husband has an affair to the emotions a man has when his wife doesn't praise him. I couldn't believe my ears! Anabel, I *never* praise my husband. I always think, *He can't do anything right.*

Last night I had a dream. I dreamed my husband had an affair, and I dreamed the *details*. I actually *felt* the emotions. It hurt so badly. I woke up at 4:30 A.M., sobbing. It was at that point I realized what I was doing to my husband . . . and God began a work in me.

The most dramatic incident I have encountered in dealing with this issue was with a couple who had been married for 13 years when they filed for divorce. The man was venting his frustration, and at the height of his tirade, he looked at his wife and said, "Never, my dear wife! Never, in 13 long years of marriage, have you ever praised me in front of anyone!" God programmed him with that desperate need for praise, and by failing to meet that need, his wife had failed in her role.

A gentleman came up to me one time after I had shared this story and asked if he could talk with me. I guess he was in his mid-sixties, and it was interesting to me that he had a hat in his hands. He would look down, twist the hat, then look up to talk to me. This was what he said: "You remember the man whose wife had not praised him in 13 years, Anabel?" "Yes," I said. He twisted his hat, looked up, then down again. There were tears in his eyes. When he regained his composure, he continued.

"Would you believe *39 years*, Anabel?"

"I beg your pardon?"

"Yes. Thirty-nine long years . . ."

I talked to him for quite a while. He told me that his wife had never been content with him, that he had tried to please her but just couldn't seem to meet her standards. Then, as though he were confessing to someone who could forgive him, he told me how he had visited his sister recently for a month, alone. His wife chose not to go with him. While he was there, he went to a senior citizens barbecue and sat by a woman who simply listened to him and responded to him with pleasant words and interesting questions. They saw each other several times during his visit. "We never touched each other, and I can't explain what happened to me when we were together . . . walking, talking, sitting at a card table drinking coffee. I was content. I was special. I didn't entertain any ideas about leaving my wife, Anabel. I would never do that. But it was awfully hard to go back home."

This is not an example of the "sick, male ego." It is a God-given need. Men need praise from the women in their lives, starting with mother, continuing with wife, and ending with death! Don't be fooled into thinking, *Don't they ever grow up?* It's the same with us. After all, we never get so old that we don't need to feel feminine.

I was visiting my 96-year-old auntie in California. We were shopping for some lingerie—a bra. I had never seen a 96-year-old body, and I must confess I was shocked.

It seemed to be one big wrinkle, void of any firmness in any area.

Well, I chose several styles and took them to the dressing room for her fitting and approval. She began vetoing them at once. I was curious. "What's wrong with these, Blanchie?"

"Oh, Honey, I want something with lace on it!"

Your husband's need of value, his sense of identity, is just as intense as yours. Ask God to instill in you a sensitivity to his need for praise, ask Him to empower you to meet this need in your husband's life. I promise He will do it.

Mission Impossible? No!

Do you remember from Chapter 1 the verse I shared from Ephesians? The verse that seemed impossible for me to carry out?

> Let the wife see that she respects and reverences her husband—that she notices him, regards him, honors him, prefers him, venerates and esteems him; and that she defers to him, praises him, and loves and admires him exceedingly (5:33b, AMP).

I had no idea how to begin putting this verse into practice. How could I praise my husband when I didn't even like him? After recognizing that Christ was my life and that He wanted to live that verse through me, it didn't seem nearly so impossible. The responsibility was His. Trusting Him to do it through me, I began to notice the things Bill did and praised him for them. (This wasn't to manipulate him or to get him to perform the way I wanted him to perform. It was obedience to God; it was fulfilling my role.) And I could tell Bill noticed, too.

I think of the man who loved to grow African violets. His wife ridiculed him—they "took up too much room" and were "messy." He literally glowed when I asked him questions, showing interest in his flowers. It made him feel important because of his achievement.

And there was Dad—how protective he was of me. We were at a high school football game, and there were two men sitting on the bleachers behind us who were drunk. They were being loud and crude. Dad was not a big man, but he challenged them both and told them to leave or shut up, that he was not going to allow that kind of language in front of his daughter. The men left, and I held his hand tightly. He was my protector.

I remember the time my sister and I had car trouble and were stranded in Atoka, Oklahoma. I visited with a couple of the mechanics while Betty apprised her husband of the situation over the phone. I told the mechanics how completely inept I was when my car decided to have an attack of some kind, and how Mother had carried one of Dad's hats in the rear window of the car for years after he was gone. It gave her a sense of security; it made a statement: There's a man around somewhere. There's his hat in the rear window.

"We depend on you men a lot," I said. "But then, I guess you know that."

One of them punched the other in the ribs and said, "I like that."

I wasn't trying to impress them. I wasn't "playing up to them." I was letting them know they were special people. There's nothing that rivals God's creation, the male. What beautiful creatures they are! What fun they have! How nice it is to have them around, especially as a part of our lives—to love us.

Your husband may have been programmed to feel unworthy of praise. (Do you remember that you will *feel* like what you set your mind on?) That's one of his flesh patterns, and we'd have to sit and talk a while to find out why it's there. For whatever reasons, he truly believes that anyone who considers him worth anything must have lost his marbles! He's uncomfortable when he's in the role of leadership. He has believed this since he was a child, and it's up to you (allowing God to work through you in the power of the Holy Spirit) to help him build new patterns.

Packaged inside your praise must be his freedom to fail. Encourage him to share with you. Ask him questions. Show interest in what he's doing and how he's doing it. And when he experiences failure—listen and sympathize and edify, and listen and sympathize and edify. (Notice that "advice" is not listed. Give it only upon request and then with gentle tact and admiration. He needs someone to stand by him, to walk with him and affirm his sense of self-worth. He needs you on his side.)

The Men in My Life

First, there was my daddy; what a wonderful man he was! How I admired him! Then I met Jesus, but I didn't spend any time with Him. I didn't know Him. He was just a male acquaintance. Then along came Bill, and man's reputation was blighted for a while. But those early years with Bill forced me to spend time with that other man in my life, Jesus. How thankful I am for those years that brought me to Him! And for the husband I now have. Oh, he's still "just my Bill," but he's as precious a husband and friend as any woman could ever dream of having. Only Jesus could have mended what was so badly broken—broken beyond *my* ability to repair.

Perhaps the men in your life have left a lot to be desired, and you're not quite sure the man in your life now is worth all this effort. I understand. But if you'd like to see the finished product, if you want to know what God had in mind when He molded the creature, then look at Jesus Christ, the perfect Man. Tender. Strong. Concerned. He loves you so much that He gave His life for you. That is man in his finest hour.

> How do I love thee? Let me count the ways.
> I love thee to the depth and breadth and height
> My soul can reach, when feeling out of sight
> For the ends of Being and ideal Grace.
> I love thee to the level of everyday's
> Most quiet need, by sun and candle-light.
> I love thee freely, as men strive for Right;
> I love thee purely, as they turn from Praise.
> I love thee with the passion put to use
> In my old griefs, and with my childhood's faith.
> I love thee with a love I seemed to lose
> With my lost saints,—I love thee with the breath,
> Smiles, tears, of all my life!—and, if God choose,
> I shall but love thee better after death.
>
> —Elizabeth Barrett Browning

For You

Do you feel neglected? "Look, I have needs, too. I'm giving and not getting. My tub is draining, and there's no water going in! This is *not* a good deal. You have not written a single line suggesting that *he* do anything other than just bask in all you've given me to do! I can't believe this is what God intended."

Think through all the time we've spent together, the

things we've shared. I began our time together by saying, "I love you. I give myself to you." When you truly love someone, you want her to have a rich, full, and happy life, and you will do whatever is within your power to see her come to know a life that is full and rich and happy. I've intentionally not mentioned your needs. There's one chapter left—it's for you.

13

The One Chapter Left

The dove has neither claw nor sting
Nor weapon for the fight.
She owes her safety to the wing
Her victory to flight.
The Bridegroom opens
His arms of love
And in them folds the panting dove
Betrothed—eternally.

Marcus was gone. They had worked in the garden together all morning, and after lunch Jean left to run a few errands. He stayed home to sit in his favorite lawn chair in the side yard under the shade tree. He was still there in his chair, in the yard and under the tree, when she pulled into the driveway. But he was gone—a massive coronary, their fiftieth wedding anniversary only months away.

Dad had retired early, and he and Mother had become so close that once she was left without him—a change so traumatic and radical—adjustment seemed virtually impossible. No more picnics with a thermos of hot coffee; no more long drives on forgotten roads to nostalgic places; no more walks in the country; no more Friday evening trips to Ft. Smith for supper at Luby's Cafeteria. Mother was alone, and I watched and tried to help as she struggled to find reason in living.

"Let's go shopping, Mother."

"Oh, Honey, I don't really want to. I don't have anyone to dress for anymore."

I would inspect the refrigerator: "Mother, are you eating well? This icebox is bare."

"I just don't enjoy cooking anymore, Anabel. Besides, I'm not very hungry."

In an effort to find some relief, Mother went to California to visit her sister, Blanchie, and began going to some senior citizens gatherings. It was there that she met a "delightful man" named Paul. The news was progressive.

"*We* saw Paul at the meeting today. He is such a nice person."

"Paul took *us* to dinner this evening."

"*Paul and I* went to the beach yesterday for a picnic. It seems like such a long time since I've had so much fun!"

"Paul took *me* to dinner tonight."

Final message: "I'm coming home to talk with you about Paul."

Bill and I drove to Poteau to meet Mother. (We had

grown up, met and married there, and Mother lived in the brick house just down from the Nazarene Church and two blocks from the old high school.) We arrived ahead of schedule and, quite unexpectedly, saw her downtown. She was making some last-minute purchases for our homecoming and was crossing the street to Holton's grocery store.

I wasn't ready for the amazing change that had taken place in Mother's appearance. She looked years younger! There was a sparkle in her eyes, a soft flush on her cheeks, and she had been shopping (her new dress had a slightly shorter hemline). *She walked with the poise and confidence of a woman who knows she is loved.* You see, her needs were being met once more. There was someone who thought she was pretty; there was someone who needed her, accepted her, and gave her life purpose and meaning; there was that special someone who loved her.

My life changed dramatically once I realized and accepted God's unconditional love as He revealed it to me so poignantly through precious Mason. Like Mother, I knew there was that special Someone who loved me. And yet, there remained a deep, inner longing for someone who *needed* me, who considered *me* special, who gave my life purpose and meaning. Those needs were not being met by my husband; he was still struggling to survive himself.

You see, even though I had come to realize that God's love for me was unconditional, I had yet to discover the *relevance* of His love in my life. I had yet to grasp His love on a practical level, on an intimate level. I had yet to realize that a relationship with Him meant talking with Him, being with Him, having fellowship with Him on an every-moment-of-every-day basis, and having my needs met by Him.

All: Every Part or Bit; Totality

In his letter to the Philippians, Paul wrote, "My God shall supply all your needs according to His riches in glory in Christ Jesus" (4:19).

For many years, I considered those "needs" to be the ones we ordinarily anticipate being met or we earnestly pray for: mainly physical comforts, like a house and a car, financial needs, health and healing, comfort in death, strength for the day, and so forth. But *all* my needs? He can meet every one of them? Yes, that's what the verse says; and yet, I dare say some of you may think I am way out in left field by suggesting that God can meet *all* your needs as a woman.

"Oh, I believe He can meet those *other* needs," you might say, "but really now, my need

- ". . . to be loved by another *person*—that void that at times engulfs me and leaves me in a helpless, hopeless heap?
- ". . . for companionship—someone to enjoy life with, like Marcus and Jean: picnics, drives down forgotten roads, walks in the country, and supper at Luby's?
- ". . . for someone to know my pain and to sincerely care—to listen and understand?
- ". . . to be appreciated and accepted as I am?
- ". . . to be needed? To be fulfilled?

"These needs? Anabel, I just can't believe this is God's plan; I mean, I guess He could do that if He wanted to, but these needs are to be met by a husband, not by God."

Wait a moment. Isn't God the one who created you with these needs?

"Yes, He is."

Do you mean to imply, then, that He is incapable of meeting them? That you must depend on someone else to meet these needs? That *you* must cope with them, live with them, accept them as your lot in life, and ultimately die with them?

That bursts the balloon, doesn't it? If you have a need God cannot meet, then He is not omnipotent, is He? *If He can't meet every need, then He's not who He claims to be—God.* Let me put it another way: God created me, female, as a part of a whole (don't stop reading, single person); consequently, He placed within me certain needs that are to be met by the *other* part of that whole, the male. But when we are denied that provision by the death of our husband, by divorce, by singleness, or by a husband who is ignorant of or rebellious in his role, God is able to fill that void and to meet those needs. He is able to complete His own creation.

Is the lonely, single woman forgotten? Isolated?

> "All I ever wanted was to have kids, to have a family, to have someone there when I got home."

Is the divorcée judged and left wanting? Wounded? Hurting?

> "How can I be Mom, Dad, provider, coach, and homemaker all at once? How can I be the glue that holds it all together when I'm coming unglued myself? I need someone. . . ."

Is the widow to endure loneliness and loss of direction for the rest of her life?

"I don't have anyone who cares anymore. 'm alone, you see."

Is the woman unhappily married destined never to realize the joy of sharing life with a loving companion?

"I see other couples holding hands and laughing together, going to movies or walking in the mall, and here I am in a relationship that's supposed to meet all my needs. What a laugh! We are two lonely people living together—and hating it."

He Is

When God met with Moses prior to the exodus, He identified Himself as, "I am who I am" (Exodus 3:14). With this declaration, God not only established His eternal sovereignty, but He also let Moses know:

- I am all that you need Me to be.
- I am the source that is able to fill the deepest void.
- I am the peace and the hope in living.
- I am the love greater than any loneliness or pain.
- I am the contentment beyond all comprehension.
- I am there for you.

He Is There

When you plumb the depths of God's "being there" to meet our every need, you discover an intimate relationship, a oneness. Do you remember Paul's reference to the body when he clarified the relationship between Christ and man?

Husbands, love your wives, just as Christ also loved the church and gave Himself up for her; that He might sanctify her, having cleansed her by the washing of water with the word, that He might present to Himself the church in all her glory, having no spot or wrinkle or any such thing; but that she should be holy and blameless. . . . For no one ever hated his own flesh, but nourishes and cherishes it, just as Christ also does the church, because we are members of His body (Ephesians 5:25-27, 29, 30).

According to the verses above,

- Who is the Husband? Jesus.
- Who is the wife? The church.
- Who makes up the church? You, as a believer; me, as a believer.

Concerning your personal relationship with Christ, do you consider yourself simply one among the many? Or is your attitude one of, "He died for *me!* 'I am my Beloved's and He is mine.' He loves *me.*"

Well, you are a part of the whole, but you are also unique, special, a "one of a kind." Would it be wrong, then, to think of *yourself* as the bride of Christ? Of course not! Jesus did not come to indwell the church; He came to indwell the individual, the believer. He came to indwell *you* (1 John 4:15). Yes, you were created to be a part of a whole, and, yes, your husband was designed to be the other half of that whole. This is the ideal in marriage, but, more often than not, the ideal is far from the norm.

My dear one, please listen. The physical arms of Jesus are not there to hold you. You are limited in your ability to see Him, to touch Him, to hear Him—but *He is there*, and your relationship with Him will only be as real as you allow it to be. Throughout Scripture, we are reminded to:

- "Stay our minds on Him" (Isaiah 26:3).
- "Abide in [Christ]" (John 15:4).
- "Set [our] minds on things above" (Colossians 3:2).
- "Dwell on these things" (Philippians 4:8).

Through setting your mind on who you are in Christ—

- His unconditional love for you
- His constant presence with you
- Your noble calling as His bride
- His promises of love and encouragement
- His thoughtfulness
- His tenderness
- His complete commitment to you

—you will begin to *experience* His intimate love in your life.

Jesus longs for our relationship with Him to be intimate and personal, a husband/wife relationship. Isaiah wrote, "For your husband is your Maker, Whose name is the LORD of hosts" (54:5). And Hosea prophesied about our relationship with God:

> "And it will come about in that day [the day of the New Covenant]," declares the LORD, "That you will call Me *Ishi* [my husband], and will no longer call Me *Baali* [my owner]. . . . And I will betroth you [a binding agreement] to Me forever; Yes, I will betroth you to Me in

righteousness and in justice, in lovingkindness and in compassion, and I will betroth you to Me in faithfulness. Then you will *know* the LORD" (2:16,19,20, emphasis added).

Did you comprehend those incredible words? Words written to you? For you? About you?

- forever
- righteousness
- justice
- love
- kindness
- compassion
- faithfulness

Whatever your status may be—married, single, divorced, widowed—you need someone who will not strike out and hurt; someone to understand you, to hold you, and to need you; someone who thinks you are beautiful, who loves you in spite of your faults, and who gently corrects you when you fail. You need someone to whom you are special, who enables you to walk down the street thinking, *I am loved! I am needed! There is someone walking with me, and there is someone waiting for me when I get home. I'm not alone anymore.* And once you have that someone in your life, you begin to live enveloped in that radiant glow, that confidence, which surrounds the woman who knows she is loved. My sister, you are a beloved bride, and you have all these needs met in your Husband, Jesus Christ!

"All right, Anabel, I see what you're saying, and I believe it's true. But tell me this: How does the satisfaction of these needs become a practical reality in my life?" Yes, that's the important issue, isn't it? You don't have a husband, or you have a husband who isn't meeting your needs, and you're alone, you're lonely, you're hurting.

How God Meets Your Needs

It was snowing—cold and windy—and I was traveling alone. I was going to Poteau to spend a few days with Mother. My bus had arrived late in Muskogee, and making the next connection was going to be close. *If only Bill were here to take care of my luggage,* I thought. I stopped a redcap and asked him if he would see about getting my things transferred. He'd had a bad day, I suppose, because he curtly informed me that he was busy and would help if he had the time.

Then came the familiar drone: "All passengers continuing to Westville, Stilwell, Poteau, and points beyond, please load at Dock #3."

I reluctantly climbed on. As I sat looking out my window at the mountain of bags, wondering where mine were, I began thinking, *Bill isn't here, but my heavenly Husband is with me. If Bill were here, I would be relaxed, trusting him to handle this problem; but here I am, all uptight, thinking I'm all alone and not trusting Jesus to take care of me.* I deliberately turned from the window and began to trust Him, thanking Him for being with me, for watching over me, and for meeting my needs. Even when the driver revved up the engine, I refused to panic. Just then, the front door of the bus opened and my redcap friend appeared. He began scanning the people and finally caught my attention. He gave me the "all's well" sign, smiled, and stepped off the bus.

Elementary, isn't it? Something I should have been able to handle, right? Wrong. I have a Husband who meets my every need, including that of getting my luggage on the bus! But first, I had to *choose* to trust Him implicitly and *allow* Him to meet my need. And had my luggage not made it onto the bus in spite of my trust in Him? My needs still would have been met, for the promise remains the same: "My God shall supply all your needs."

A friend of mine had been happy in her marriage and was much too young to be a widow. But Dave was gone now, and she was alone. She had never imagined the day would come when he would no longer walk through the door and say, "Hi, Sweetie. It's nice to come home to you—did you know that?" No, she was totally unprepared for such an event in her life.

How do I continue? she would wonder. *This void, this loneliness, this loss of direction and purpose—God, how can everything keep running? I hear the clock, the refrigerator, the air conditioner—how am I to keep going?*

The days passed. She came across an emerald ring her grandmother had given her years ago. When Dave had given her her wedding bands, she had taken the emerald off and worn it only on special occasions. As it happened, this night turned out to be a very special occasion.

The day had been a lonely one; that night, kneeling by her bed, she took her wedding rings off and held them tightly in her fist. She fought the memories swirling through her mind. Then slowly, deliberately, she put the bands on her right ring finger, and she prayed: "Lord, You are now my Husband in a way that You have never been before. Dave was here, but he's gone now. With this emerald ring, I enter into a new covenant with You, a new marriage agreement, a new union, a new beginning. I ask You to fulfill my life with Your love."

The ring slipped on easily.

Now, as she shares this beautiful story, she holds out her hand and reminds me, "See, Anabel? I'm not a widow—and I never will be. There will always be Someone who thinks it's 'neat' to come home to me."

Another woman told me of her encounter with the Man of her dreams:

> Anabel, I'm 41 years old and single, not that I'm ashamed of being single. I just never thought that this would be my lot in life, and for years I resented the loneliness, the weariness, the responsibility. I "claimed" a husband, drew up my image of him, anticipated his coming into my life every day, and went to every function with great expectations.
>
> You get tired of expecting. You get tired of trying to look nice when no one ever seems to notice. You get tired of cooking for one. You just get tired of your life and there doesn't seem to be any way out.
>
> But not any more. I now walk with the poise and confidence of a woman who knows she is loved—loved by her Savior. I cannot express to you the joy and contentment that has come into my life as the bride of such a Husband as I do have. I had to practice. I had to learn to live with Him. But don't all married people have to adjust to another presence in their every-moment world?
>
> He is so real to me now, such an integral part of my life, that I am never alone. I have discovered the truth of what you said, "He will be just as real to you as you will allow Him to be."

I'm not going to say that I can control my emotions, but then, they are not the barometer of Truth, are they? I know how to deal with my loneliness, my disillusionment, my depression, my independence, my need for masculine approval. I have a Husband. A Husband who loves me more dearly and faithfully than any earthly husband could ever love me.

Thank you for introducing me to Him. You're quite a "matchmaker"!

He Knows, He Cares

Do you need to feel loved? To feel needed? To feel secure?

You have seen me tossing and turning through the night. You have collected all my tears and preserved them in your bottle! You have recorded them in your book (Psalm 56:8, TLB).

O LORD, YOU have examined my heart and know everything about me. You know when I sit or stand. When far away you know my every thought. You chart the path ahead of me, and tell me where to stop and rest. Every moment, you know where I am (Psalm 139:1-3, TLB).

How precious it is, Lord, to realize that you are thinking about me constantly. I can't even count how many times a day your thoughts turn towards me. And when I waken in the morning, you are still thinking of me! (Psalm 139:17,18, TLB).

So you're wearing a new dress, and your husband doesn't notice? Listen. You will "hear" Jesus say, "You look so pretty."

You've worked hard, and the house is spotless. The furniture is all moved around, and everything smells clean and looks great! Your husband doesn't even seem to care. Listen. You will hear Jesus say, "How nice the house looks. You do a great job; I'm proud of you."

Do you need tenderness, to be understood? Do you long for someone to hear you, to listen to you? Try Him.

Have you done it all wrong? Have you failed, and do you need someone to encourage you, to help you? Try Him.

Many times, after he has been away, Bill will bring me a little knickknack he has found somewhere and bought for me. Do you know what that says to me? "I was thinking about you, and when I saw this, I couldn't resist bringing it to you."

I *need* that, and it isn't that I need the gift so much, but I need the evidence of what the gift is saying: *I was thinking of you, and here's something to prove it.*

The Bible says that the Lord notices when even a sparrow falls, that He charts the course of the wild goose, that He orders the steps of the righteous man, and that He knew us before the foundation of the world. He is always aware of us, thinking of us and of our every need.

So, those beautiful sunsets—I *receive* them as a gift from my spiritual Husband: "Lord, if You're not the most thoughtful person; Your creativity just amazes me. You never cease to come up with new ways to let me know that I'm special to You. What a joy it is to be Your bride."

I receive the lightning and the rainstorms. I receive the neat rows of red apples at the market and the job I go to each day. I receive the tree alive with pecans and my silly dog, Bo, charging around the backyard. All these I accept as love gifts from my Husband, Jesus, to me: "I was thinking about you, and I wanted you to know."

Are You Married?

God's plan is for you and your husband to complete one another and to come to know the incredible oneness that only He can bring into your lives. In many cases, however, the marriage relationship is one of starvation and deprivation where crucial needs are left desperately wanting. *Jesus is able to meet your every need in such circumstances,* but your relationship with Him should not exclude your husband. Christ *in* you will be aware of every need in your husband's life, and He desires to meet those needs through you. And as for you? Live in the promise of Jesus' unconditional love; revel in being His beloved, His bride.

Are You Alone?

I can't promise you that someone else will come into your life, but you can be assured of this: *God's love for you is unequivocally true, unchanging, and eternal. Your relationship with Him is indestructible and will endure for eternity.*

My prayer is that God will reveal to you the exquisite truth that you do not have to live life lonely, feeling unloved, believing that you are unneeded and unappreciated. He is there. He is whatever you need Him to be, dear one, and He is faithful—*forever.*

Lovingly,
Anabel

Jesus, the Groom

My love extends to the heavens
I give you My love
My faithfulness reaches to the skies
I will be faithful to you
I gave Myself for you long ago
I have loved you from before the birth of time
Every path that you walk will be fragrant
With My lovingkindness and My truth
I promise to be patient and kind
To never be selfish or rude
I will not demand My own way

Nor will I be irritable or touchy
I will not hold a grudge against you
Even if you should treat Me shabbily
I will delight in your love
I will be loyal to you
Even if everyone else should abandon you
I will always believe in you
And I will never leave you or forsake you
I promise you these things
And I do not lie
Seek Me first
Love Me above all others

And I will take care of you
I will meet your every need
These things I declare
I will keep these promises
Which I have sworn to you
For I am faithful . . . forever

You, the Bride

My precious Jesus
I take You to be my wedded Husband
For richer or for poorer
In sickness and in health
To have and to hold as long as we both shall live
Which is for all eternity

I hereby give myself to You
And I do so gladly
Willingly
And with no regrets
I do not pause to look back for what might have been
Or for those things I never knew

In Your hands there are scars
They will always remind me of Your love for me
And how You have proven Yourself to me
This is too marvelous, too wonderful
for me to comprehend

Thank You, my Jesus, my Husband
I love you and I will be faithful to You
I am so thankful that nothing can separate us
For even death will serve only to unite us

Study Guide

Twelve Weeks of Discovering What It Means to Be God's Confident Woman

This study is designed to help you dig a little deeper into the truths shared in *The Confident Woman* and especially to help you experience these truths in your own life. You may use this guide either as an aid for personal reflection and growth or as a discussion motivator and resource tool for a study and sharing group. (A teacher's guide is available from Gillham Ministries. For more information, please call 1-800-328-6662.)

To get the most out of your study, you will need the following tools:

- a Bible
- a divided notebook
- a pen or pencil

Before you start the study, divide your notebook into three sections:

1. The first section will be used to write down your responses to the questions in the study guide.
2. The second section will be used as a journal in which to record your thoughts and prayers over the next 12 weeks.
3. The third section will be used to record key Scriptures and truths to be read daily. If you make a habit of reviewing these each day over the next 12 weeks, they will become a part of your life.

Each week's questions fall into two parts. The first contains content questions to help you review and understand what you have read (*About What You Read. . .*). The second section probes deeply into your personal opinions and feelings, and suggests activities that will help you move closer to being God's confident woman (*About You and Your Life. . .*).

If you use this book in a study group, be very sensitive to the personal nature of some of the questions. Sharing should be optional; no group member should ever feel pressured to answer questions aloud. In addition, the group should agree ahead of time to keep anything that is shared confidential.

How we pray that this time of study will be a life-changing experience for you! It can be. Your commitment and your desire will be the key. Ask God to create the desire, to carry through on your commitment, to reveal truth to you, and to cause it to bear fruit in your life.

Chapter 1
Where Horses Belong

About What You Read . . .

1. What is the central message of the "horse and cart" analogy that opens this chapter?

2. What circumstance in her life does Anabel list as her Waterloo—the situation that finally brought her to the end of her impressive but self-defeating "strength"?

3. What is the crucial first step to exploring our role as women? What happens if we ignore that step?

4. What is the "basic plan, the rudimentary principle of His original intent"?

About You and Your Life . . .

5. Which of the following responses comes closest to your personal response as you read the introduction and the first chapter:

   A. This woman needs help! I may not be perfect, but at least I'm in better shape than she was!

   B. She's just like me! Anabel's story is the story of my life!

   C. I'm not sure I can relate to Anabel's particular problems, but I've sure got some of my own!

   D. Yes, but . . .

(Even if you don't specifically relate to Anabel's problems, keep reading. You may learn some things about yourself.)

6. In a paragraph or two, summarize the circumstances of your life right now. Include both facts ("I'm single.") and feelings ("I hate my boss!"). Feel free to gripe or complain if that's the way you feel; use this exercise to bring both your circumstances and your feelings into sharper focus. Under this paragraph, leave about ten lines of blank space. We'll be adding to it later.

7. Have you ever had the experience of coming to the end of your strength as Anabel describes? If so, what brought you there? If not, what are the areas that bring intense stress into your life and that, given the right circumstances, could possibly push you over the edge?

8. Turn to the third section of your notebook and write out John 15:5 from a translation you find most helpful. Every day for the next week, set aside a time to read that verse aloud three times. Then, in the journal section of your notebook, record the thoughts and reactions that come to you.

Chapter 2
Somebody Loves Me

About What You Read . . .

1. What is the main flaw of the "Lone Ranger" philosophy or the "I can do it myself!" theology?

2. Anabel's favorite saying was: "God helps those who help themselves." What's wrong with this theology to which she clung tenaciously?

3. If we are to experience the fullness of God's plan for our lives and to really know Him, what three areas must be totally given to Him?

4. What is the point of Anabel's story about her son Mason?

5. How does God love you, His child? Why does He love you this way? Do you deserve this type of love? Does He love you anyway? What can you do to cause God to love you less? What can you do to cause God to love you more?

About You and Your Life . . .

6. In your journal section, jot down some situation in which you now realize you relied more on self than on God. How important is your performance to the way you feel about yourself?

7. Think of the people closest to you—family, friends, coworkers. Do you feel responsible for improving the adverse circumstances in their lives? How does this affect your love for them?

8. Think of a recent time when you felt totally unattractive and unlovable. With that image in mind, picture yourself in Mason's chair with Jesus kneeling before you, holding your hands. Listen carefully as He says, "(Your name), I love you. I love you! If only you could understand how very much I love you—*just because you're Mine....*"

9. On the same page in your notebook where you wrote out John 15:5, write out Ephesians 3:17-19. Every day for the next week, read *all* these verses aloud and record your thoughts in the journal section of your notebook.

Chapter 3
The Simple Truth

About What You Read . . .

1. According to Anabel, what is the one overwhelming need with which we come into the world?

2. What is Anabel's definition of the biblical concept of "flesh"?

3. Anabel describes how she went from one pattern of "flesh" (performance) to another (depression). She says: "Throughout the desperate extremes of this entire crisis situation, I never turned away from God." Why, then, did her faith not help her? Describe the turning point in this situation.

4. When did the "crucifixion" take place in Anabel's life? (Careful, this one is tricky!) Explain how this is true.

5. Dissect Galatians 2:20: *"I have been crucified with Christ."*

   To whom is this "I" referring? How many sins had you committed at the time of Christ's crucifixion? How many sins were forgiven in the year A.D. 33 at Christ's crucifixion?

   "It is no longer I who live, but Christ lives in me." What has happened to the other "me"—the one who "no longer lives"? *"And the life that I [Which "I"?] now live in the flesh, I [Which "I"?] live by faith in the Son of God, who loved me, and delivered Himself up for me."* How do you live this life in Christ?

6. According to this chapter, how does being born in Christ release you from being controlled by your unique version of the flesh?

About You and Your Life . . .

7. Anabel makes this statement: "When you are 'in Christ' (have invited Him into your heart), your whole history changes." In your journal section, write down the changes that have occurred in your life. Briefly describe in your own words what each one means to you.

8. If you are married or have been married, did Anabel's description of Bill before and after marriage spark any painful memories? How was your husband different before you married him than he was one year afterward? Did you think you could change him? Did you change him?

9. Knowing now that "birth determines identity," work through the *Personal Reflections* section of this chapter, looking up the Scriptures and applying them to your own experience. Rephrase each Scripture using the "I" pronoun to express who you *were* in Satan's family and who you *are* now as a member of God's family. Fill in the blanks for your "birth dates" and, if appropriate, sign in the designated places.

10. If you are in a private place, try following Anabel's example of lying prone in a "crucified" position. Pray your own version of the prayer on pp. 47-48. Afterward, spend some time writing down in your journal section how you felt.

11. In section three of your notebook, write down the simple little phrase that God spoke to Anabel in the quiet of her bedroom: "I will do it all for you." Write it seven times, emphasizing a different word each time:

> *I* will do it all for you.
> I *will* do it all for you.
> I will *do* it all for you.
> I will do *it* all for you.
> I will do it *all* for you.
> I will do it all *for* you.
> I will do it all for *you.*

12. Also in section three of your notebook, write the text of Galatians 2:20. Read it and the other truths in this section aloud each day this week and write down your reflections in your journal.

Chapter 4
Reprogramming Your Personal Computer

About What You Read . . .

1. According to 1 Thessalonians 5:23, every person is made up of three integrated parts. Briefly explain each of these parts as they are defined in this chapter.

2. To which part of a person does the brain belong? What part is the "seat of your personality"? Are your mind and your brain the same thing?

3. Where do "facts" originate? Where do "feelings" originate? Why is it so difficult to accept "facts" when you don't "feel" they are true in your life?

4. How does the mind influence your emotions? How do your beliefs affect your emotions and your behavior?

5. Are you under the control of your mind? Are you under the control of your emotions? Can you, with your will, *choose* to override your mind (what you *think* you should do) and your emotions (what you *feel* you should do)?

6. What is the difference between a "sinner saved by grace" and a "saint who sins"? Why is it possible to be a new person in Christ and yet continue to feel and act in ways that don't reflect that new identity?

7. As you appropriate your new identity in Christ, you will begin walking in the Spirit! Will this be an overnight change? Will you automatically "feel" like the new creature you are? According to 2 Corinthians 5:7, how must we walk?

8. According to this chapter, what two things will determine the measure of success you experience in reprogramming old habit patterns?

About You and Your Life . . .

9. In the journal section of your notebook, write out the seven undeniable facts about your identity as a "saint." (Hint: Check the subheads on pp. 68-69.) Write each one down using first-person pronouns (example: "Christ lives in me!") and explain what it means to you.

10. Reflect on your childhood: With whom did you live? What was your household like? How often do you remember being blessed with concrete and specific expressions of love? Pray for insight to understand the way your environment has shaped your flesh patterns—and for the grace, if necessary, to forgive those who failed to give you what you needed.

11. Using the *Flesh Inventory* (pp. 69-71), analyze your own version of the "flesh." Then, as honestly as you can, answer these questions: What are your "habit patterns"? What techniques have you developed for getting love or for coping with not being loved? How do you "spell" love? Up to this point, how successful have these techniques been? Write your answers in the journal section of your notebook.

Now claim 2 Corinthians 5:17 and praise God that "in Christ" you are free from these patterns! You do not have to be controlled by them any longer! *You are free!*

12. In your journal section, paraphrase Hebrews 10:16-18 in the form of a letter from God to you. (For example: "Dear _____, This is the covenant I will make with you. . . .") After a day or two, read this letter again and let its message sink into your heart.

13. What are some practical steps you can take to live according to the reality of your new, true identity rather than being controlled by your "feelings"?

14. In section three of your notebook, write out 2 Corinthians 5:17 and Romans 12:2. Each day, read these and the other truths in this section aloud. In addition, take time to look up at least some of the many Scriptures describing your true identity in Christ (pp. 72-76). Pick out one or two that are especially meaningful to you and write them out.

Chapter 5
Steps and Exits

About What You Read . . .

1. How, according to this chapter, can we be new creatures in Christ and still end up doing the very thing we hate?

2. Is a new creation in Christ (with the very *mind* of Christ [1 Corinthians 2:16b]) capable of generating negative, destructive thoughts? Who, then, is the originator of such thoughts? What does John call him in Revelation 12:9?

3. What is Satan's primary goal regarding Christians? Where does he play out his mighty war?

4. If we do not generate sinful thoughts in our minds, at what point do we become responsible for sinning?

5. On our own, are we humans capable of withstanding Satan's onslaught on our minds? What is the vital initial move we must make before Christ begins fighting that battle for us?

6. Why does Anabel state that the fight between good and evil in us is "not a civil war"? Why is this so important?

7. Why does Satan use first-person singular pronouns in giving us his thoughts? Why are these thoughts so familiar to us?

8. Name two practical strategies Anabel suggests for

exposing the thoughts Satan gives us.

9. Why is it critical to intercept harmful and deceptive thoughts at the "threshold of the mind"?

10. What are the four steps Anabel spells out for dealing with the power of sin in our lives?

About You and Your Life . . .

11. Read Romans 7:15–8:1. In the journal section of your notebook, summarize what these verses say to you.

12. Look back at the list of "seven undeniable facts" you wrote down from the last chapter. For each one, think of a lie which Satan could introduce in your mind to keep you from living fully as a new creation. When possible, try to use lies he has used on you personally. Record these in the journal section of your notebook. For example:

   God's Truths   Satan's Lies
   Christ lives in me. I'm no good to anybody.

13. What is one area in your life where you feel you have been fighting a losing battle against the "power of sin"? What two specific things can you do to have victory in this area?

14. Monitor your "self-talk" for the next few days. Try to become aware of the "I" statements you make to yourself. If you can, actually write down a typical transcript of the deceptive but familiar thoughts that tend to pull you away from what you know to be true.

15. Think of a bad habit or debilitating habit pattern, little or big, that has tripped you up repeatedly in the past. Following Anabel's example, write out a step-by-step scenario for your descent into that harmful pattern. What choices will you have to make to fall into that pattern again? Write the first three of these choices on a card along with 2 Corinthians 5:21. Put the card in your purse or in a place where you are likely to see it when temptation confronts you. Pray specifically that God will be your strength in the ongoing battle against the power of sin in your life.

16. In section three of your notebook, write down 1 Corinthians 10:13 and Romans 6:12. Continue the daily practice of reading through the truths you have written in this section.

Chapters 6 and 7
Love Letters and Envelopes
That's Not What I Meant!

Chapter 6

About What You Read . . .

1 Anabel says that theology alone is loving the "letter" (God's Word) instead of the Person who wrote the "letter" (God Himself). How can using your imagination change rows of "black print on white paper" into a love letter from the Lord?

About You and Your Life . . .

2. Make your own set of envelopes, looking up the Scriptures and writing them out on the back of each one. Go through your envelopes every day this week, praising God for this truth: "Anything that comes into my life must first come through God then through Jesus to get to me. And when it gets to me, it finds me filled with Jesus. So what is there to fear?" Write this truth in section three of your notebook.

3. Read John 14. Draw on the message of this chapter to write a letter you believe God would write to you. Be faithful to the reality of the text, but make the letter personal. Record it in the journal section of your notebook.

Chapter 7

About What You Read . . .

1. What fundamental misunderstanding was at the heart of Moses', Paul's, and Anabel's idea of how they were to reach the goal of being all that God wanted them to be?

2. What is the fundamental truth we must grasp before we can be all God wants us to be? What is the one necessary ingredient that will enable us to meet every circumstance victoriously?

About You and Your Life . . .

3. According to Anabel, what are the six signs of "being ready" to serve God? Record these in the third section of your notebook. Pray, asking God to give you understanding and to make these attitudes a part of your life.

4. Review the description of your circumstances that you wrote the first week of this study. Under that description, write out the statement: "What God wants me to be does not depend on my circumstances, the people around me, my talents, my gifts, or on making a right turn when I should have turned left." Underline that statement or mark it with a highlighter. How could the reality of this statement change the way you view your circumstances?

5. Read the prayer of commitment at the end of Chapter 7. If you aren't ready to sign it, spend time with

God, asking Him to bring you to the point of readiness.

6. Add Philippians 4:8 and Jeremiah 9:23,24 to section three of your notebook. Read them aloud daily, and write your reflections in your journal.

Chapter Eight
What to Do with Your Balloon

About What You Read . . .

1. In the journal section of your notebook, list the "six amazing facts" we have explored in the previous chapters (see pp. 135-136). Use first-person singular pronouns.

2. What is the key to being able to establish right relationships with other people?

3. What do Psalm 55:22 and 1 Peter 5:7 say we are to do with our painful circumstances, especially our painful relationships?

4. God promises to sustain us when we give Him our burdens. What kind of sustenance does Anabel indicate most of us need?

5. Why is the exercise described in this chapter so effective for making the relinquishment of our burdens to God more real? Why do we find it easier to believe what we see?

6. Does giving your burden to God in the manner described mean that you will never be unhappy, hurt, sad, or worried again? What should you do when these times come?

About You and Your Life . . .

7. Read the following statement out loud, putting your own name in the blank: "A circumstance has come

into _____'s life over which she has no control, a person she cannot control." What circumstances from your life come into your mind when you read that?

8. Plan a time this week when you will buy a balloon and give your burdens to the Lord as Anabel describes. Don't wait. He never intended for *you* to carry them!

9. Add Psalm 55:22 to section three of your notebook. Continue to read aloud the truths on these pages.

WEEK EIGHT
Chapter 9
Putting Asunder

About What You Read...

1. In what ways have our culture's attitudes toward marriage become warped? Why does Anabel believe so many young people today are living together without marriage? Do you agree?

2. According to Matthew 19:5,6, how does God view marriage?

3. List four widely held myths about divorce—general opinions that are not upheld by the facts.

4. Why is it often so difficult for adult children of divorce to make their own marriages work?

5. What, according to this chapter, is the root of the divorce problem in our culture?

About You and Your Life...

6. In what specific ways has divorce touched your life? How many people were affected? In what ways were they affected? Have any of these people *fully* recovered?

7. Look back at your parents' marriage. How did (or do) you want your marriage to be like that of your parents? How did (or do) you want it to differ? How do you think the "imprinting" or programming you were given concerning marriage has affected your attitudes and actions today?

8. If you are married, apply the same question, as best you can, to your husband's parents' marriage. In what ways have these two marriages affected your married life?

9. "In a very literal sense, I feel that I am being stripped of depending on anyone but Jesus." How would you apply that statement to the painful situations in your life—marital or otherwise? Have you known a time when you felt you were being "stripped"? Describe this in your journal.

10. Add Hebrews 13:4a to the third section of your notebook. As you read it, remember that you don't have to be married (or happily married) to hold marriage "in honor." Pray that God will heal any warped attitudes you may have picked up from experience or the general culture.

Chapter 10
Created as One

About What You Read . . .

1. List at least eight adjectives from Proverbs 31 that God uses in His definition of woman.

2. What is the only thing God created with which He was not pleased? What did He do about the problem? In Genesis 2:18, how does God describe His new creation? To whom did He give His commission?

3. What was God's name for His new creation? Who came up with the term *woman?*

4. What was God's original plan for man (both male and female) prior to the fall?

5. If men and women were meant to complement and complete each other, why does Anabel insist that a single person is *not* incomplete?

6. What one reason for the death of our Lord stands out with particular clarity?

7. Who was the first Adam? The second Adam? How are we identified with each Adam?

8. How does one person complete another in a marriage?

About You and Your Life . . .

9. Read over your list of adjectives from Proverbs 31

for "woman." How do you feel about hearing those adjectives applied to you? Why do you think you feel this way?

10. Respond to the statement, "Love does not hold a marriage together. Marriage holds love together." What do you think it means? Do you agree with it?

11. If you are married, how do you and your husband complement/complete one another? If you are single, how did your parents complement/complete one another?

12. Add 1 Corinthians 11:11 to section three of your notebook. As you read it aloud, ponder how it specifically applies in your life (whether or not you are married).

Chapter 11
One Near One Is Too Far

About What You Read . . .

1. In what four ways does God want a husband and wife to become one?

2. In which of these ways are males and females *not* different? What common need do we both have in this area?

3. Explain in your own words what Anabel means by one + one + one = one.

4. According to Philippians 2:5-8, what attitude is the essence of spiritual oneness? How can we ever manage to develop such an attitude?

5. For what end does God use "impressed forces" (heavenly sandpaper) in a person's life? If we are open to His use of heavenly sandpaper in our lives, what results may we expect from its use?

6. What, according to C.S. Lewis, is the real problem with sex outside of marriage?

7. For what reasons did God create sexual intercourse (besides reproduction)? What are some of the major differences in a man's and a woman's sexual needs?

8. What is the only way that physical oneness can be experienced in all its beauty? How is this truth being ignored in the world today?

9. What does it mean to be perceptually one? Why is this more difficult than becoming physically one? What are the limitations of this kind of oneness?

10. What five elements are necessary for developing emotional oneness? In general, which partner is better equipped for this part of a relationship?

11. In a marriage which is "not operating at maximum capacity," what is the wife's responsibility?

About You and Your Life . . .

12. Dr. Wallerstein says that "a good marriage brings about a 'new entity,' a 'new marital identity,' where each partner finds it difficult to think of himself or herself as separate from the other partner." If you are married, is this your experience? Why do you believe this is or is not true?

13. If you are married, list (and thank God for) five positive traits your husband has that are not strong traits for you. If you are not married, list five of your weak areas—areas in which you could use a completer. Then remind yourself that you *have* a Completer in your life.

14. In what ways have you experienced the "impressed force" of God molding you into the likeness of Christ? Looking back, describe your attitude during the time you were having to suffer through this experience. If you are married, what are some ways God may be using the two of you as "heavenly sandpaper" on each other?

15. Write out 2 Corinthians 3:18 in section three of your notebook. Continue your pattern of reading these truths aloud each day. Can you feel this daily habit changing you?

Chapter 12
Three Needs

About What You Read . . .

1. Name the four characteristics that will be evident as you allow Christ to live out His agape love through you.

2. What is the goal of agape love for a married woman? What positive results will a woman begin to see in her marriage as she allows Christ to love her husband through her? According to 2 Corinthians 3:5, from where will a married woman gain the strength to love her husband this way?

3. Is obedience to God's command that a wife love her husband this way conditional to whether or not her husband is a Christian? Is it conditional on his loving her or meeting her needs?

4. What three basic needs has God programmed into every human being? By meeting these needs, what does a wife communicate to her husband?

5. According to this chapter, for a wife not to accept her husband is to _____ him. What are some common ways in which wives communicate rejection to their husbands? What are ways to communicate belonging and acceptance?

6. Why is it important for a wife to work at being physically attractive to her husband? What are the three cardinal rules for a woman to remember in the physical area of her marriage?

7. "The male was programmed by God for _____." What negative results can occur (in an adult or a child) when the male's God-given role in this area is usurped?

8. Generally speaking, men and women view problems differently. Men tend to evaluate problems through their _____, while women use their _____. Which approach is superior? _____ How can these differences be used as a source of strength and not of conflict in a marriage?

9. After both spouses use their God-given abilities to evaluate and discuss a problem, whose God-given role is it to make the final decision? How can a wife give constructive advice to her husband?

10. Women are not called to leadership in the home, but to _____. When a Christian wife chooses to serve her husband, who is she ultimately serving?

11. Why is praise so important to a man? How can a woman learn to praise a man whom she doesn't even like or a man who doesn't accept praise well?

12. How should godly women respond when the men in their lives fail?

About You and Your Life . . .

13. Look up and record in the journal section of your notebook what each of the following verses says about your role as a follower of Christ:

   A. Mark 10:45
   B. Luke 4:8

      C. 1 Corinthians 10:31
      D. Galatians 5:13-16
      E. Ephesians 4:1-3

14. If you are married, think over the last few weeks. Can you think of ways in which you might have rejected your husband or indicated you value other areas of your life more than you value him? List three specific ways you can express to him that you are glad he is yours.

15. Is it hard for you to allow your husband to be the head of your home? What reasons do you think are at the root of this problem? What negative consequences are occurring in your home as a result of this disobedience?

16. What is the difference between consciously giving a man the leadership role in a relationship and being a doormat for an overbearing husband? What is the key to conceding leadership while maintaining a healthy self-image?

17. Do you find it hard to offer praise to the men in your life? Why do you think this is true? Go to the journal section of your notebook and create a column for each man who plays a substantial role in your life. Pray and ask God to show you ways you could offer praise to each of them during the coming weeks. If years of resentment or anger have built up between you and some of these men, ask God to offer this praise to them for you and through you. Then pray that He will work through you to forgive and begin building bridges of healing in the relationship. (Remember, with God, all things are possible!)

18. Write out Ephesians 5:33b in the third section of your notebook and read it out loud daily as a reminder of God's ideal for a woman's role in marriage. If you aren't married, apply the same admonition to your relationship with Christ.

Chapter 13
The One Chapter Left

About What You Read . . .

1. When God met with Moses prior to the exodus, He identified Himself as "I AM WHO I AM" (Exodus 3:14). What were some of the roles He was promising to fill?

2. According to Ephesians 5:25-30, what is the nature of the relationship between Christ and man? In the journal section of your notebook, briefly summarize these verses, seeing yourself as the church, the very bride of Christ.

3. How can Christ's love be real for us when we can't see Him, touch Him, or hear Him? Name four ways we stay close to Him.

4. Does God desire to overshadow a married woman's husband in the area of meeting her needs? What is the husband's role in this overall scheme? If there are areas of your life where your husband is not meeting your needs, what incredible, incomprehensible provision has God made for you?

About You and Your Life . . .

5. In the journal section of your notebook, write down some needs you currently have which are not being met. In Philippians 4:19, how many of your needs does our omnipotent God say He is capable of meeting?

6. Write out Philippians 4:19 as the final verse for the third section of your notebook. Open your heart to God now, thanking Him that He loves you unconditionally and is able to complete His own creation!

7. Read the vows in "Jesus, the Groom" silently, imagining God speaking these words to you. Then read aloud the vows in "You, the Bride" back to Him. Praise God for His marvelous, beautiful, wonderful plan for completing you—His beloved, confident woman.

Notes

Chapter Two

1. A.W. Tozer, *The Best of Tozer* (Grand Rapids, MI: Baker Book House, 1978), p. 120.

Chapter Three

1. Dr. Martin Bergmann, *Newsday* (November 15, 1989).

Chapter Six

1. "Love Letters." Copyright © 1945 by Famous Music Corporation. Copyright renewed 1972 by Famous Music Corporation.

Chapter Eleven

1. Vivian Gornick, *New York Times Magazine* (April 15, 1990).
2. C.S. Lewis, *Mere Christianity* (London: Collins, Limited, 1952).

Chapter Twelve

1. "Bill." Music by Jerome Kern and lyrics by Oscar Hammerstein II and Sir P.G. Wodehouse. Copyright © 1927 PolyGram International Publishing, Inc. Copyright renewed. International Copyright Secured. All Rights Reserved. Used by permission.

Aren't you glad you're still under warranty?

LIFETIME GUARANTEE

You've tried fixing your marriage, your kids, your job. Suddenly the light dawns. It's not your *problems* that need to be fixed—it's your *life*! The good news is that God doesn't ask you to live *your* life for Christ, but to let Him live *His* life through you.

With humor, candor, and "plain vanilla talk," author Bill Gillham takes a new and enlightening look at the concept of your identity *in Christ*. A Christian who walks in this manner is backed by God's lifetime guarantee.